DELUSION
A DRUG OF CHOICE

self help & case studies for mental health practitioners

by
Irene Greene Murphy
LCSW, LADC, OMC

Delusion: A Drug of Choice

©2015 Irene Greene Murphy

ISBN 13: 978-1-63381-028-0

designed and produced by
Maine Authors Publishing
558 Main Street, Rockland, Maine 04841
www.maineauthorspublishing.com

Manufactured in the United States of America

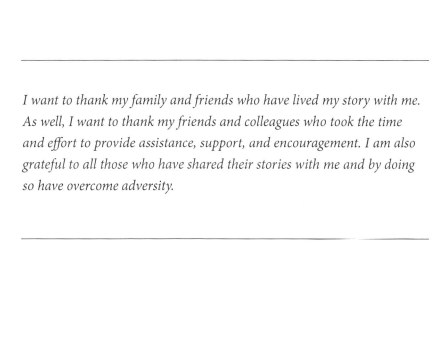

I want to thank my family and friends who have lived my story with me. As well, I want to thank my friends and colleagues who took the time and effort to provide assistance, support, and encouragement. I am also grateful to all those who have shared their stories with me and by doing so have overcome adversity.

Disclaimer

The case histories in this book are fictional and were developed from the stories of many clients over the course of 38 years of clinical work. I developed characters that may appear to be similar but are in no way based on any one client. The fictional stories were created in order to protect the confidentiality of any person they might appear to identify.

TABLE OF CONTENTS

Introduction

If you look for truth, you may find comfort in the end;
If you look for comfort you will not get either comfort or truth,
Only soft soap and wishful thinking to begin, and in the end, despair.
—C. S. Lewis

My journey has been slow, but the outcome for me is the cumulative result of many "epiphanies" that have opened my heart and allowed me to embrace my true self free from "delusion." I now love and live life honestly. It was at first external: my body, my environment, my family, my job. Then it was my mind—the internal voice that fed my delusions and took me away from truth and peace. The truth came through once I learned new skills like meditation, goal setting, patience, and planning. That was not all: a "dark side" emerged that I had never seen before and which I feared.

Only by being as brave as I could be did I find the courage to embrace my fear. I refused to allow it to cause me to overanalyze or get out of control. By doing this, I found that my fear disintegrated and a flood of peacefulness enveloped me. Then I remembered the quote from the famous psychotherapist Eric Fromm: "The task we must seek for ourselves is not to feel secure, but to be able to tolerate insecurity." As I reread this quote, I finally understood the meaning of true happiness and became clear about what had been missing within me. I wish to share with you my journey and the skills I have learned in the hope that you too may find the joy I have found.

There have been three major insights that were critical to my "awakening":

- Resentments are healed by developing an inner sense of being needed and cherished.
- Feelings of desertion and separation are healed by feelings of appreciation for my uniqueness.
- There is no such thing as having "no choice."

The more aware we become of our values, assumptions, and the extent we have been influenced by them, the more we can break bad habits that have been created from our reactions. We break out of the boxes that hold back our growth. We begin to see the delusions/distortions/lies we have let into our lives. Then and only then can we examine these delusions. By stopping and really looking, we get a more objective and panoramic view and see clearly how our delusions are affecting our lives. This is what "clarity" and "being focused" really mean. No quick looks. No quick fixes. If any response is quick, we are missing something. It isn't a response, it is a reaction, and I hope that, after reading this book, you too will know the difference. Responses are based in reality, while some "reactions" are flights into delusion. The following chapters will provide you with the tools and steps that are critical to staying grounded in reality, which is the only real way out of delusions.

~Namaste~
Irene Greene Murphy, LCSW, LADC, OMC
Mt. Desert Island, Maine

Chapter 1

Delusions in Everyday Life

The term *delusion* means different things to different people. Occasionally, you may hear the criticism "you're delusional" when someone disagrees with an idea or belief someone else has just expressed. It's meant to belittle that person by inferring that they are just plain "nuts." It refers to a point of view or thought that differs from what is considered the "norm" and therefore becomes suspect, just as the person holding the belief or idea becomes suspect by association.

But in the field of psychology and psychiatry, *delusion* means something quite different. Delusions generally come in two categories of severity: neurotic and psychotic. The difference is one of degree, but both contain the same essential features, namely that the person with the delusion believes completely the subject of his delusion despite clear evidence that his belief cannot be true. For the neurotic, his delusion may be hampering his life to some degree, but he can still function in society, though certainly in an impaired state. For the psychotic, the delusion is so overwhelming that he cannot function in society without the use of various antipsychotic medications and close psychiatric supervision, and in severe cases, institutionalization.

Psychotic Delusions

Delusions of a severe nature require psychiatric care. The most commonly recognized psychotic disorders where we find delusions are with schizophrenia, acute paranoia, manic episodes of bipolar disorder, dementia, and in severe depression. Delusions are categorized as being either "bizarre" or "non-bizarre."

In bizarre delusions such as schizophrenia, the person afflicted believes he has horns growing out of his head—something that could not happen in real life. A non-bizarre delusion is one that *could* happen in real life, but in the individual's situation would be extremely unlikely—the government is spying on him and coming to get him.

Delusions may also be identified by various common "themes," such as the delusion of control: This is a false belief that another person, group of people, or external force controls one's general thoughts, feelings, impulses, or behavior.

- Cotard delusion: This is a false belief that one does not exist or has died.

- Delusional jealousy: A person with this delusion falsely believes that a spouse or lover is having an affair, with no proof to back up their claim.

- Delusion of guilt or sin (or delusion of self-accusation): This is an ungrounded feeling of extreme remorse or guilt.

- Delusion of mind being read: The false belief that other people can know one's thoughts.

- Delusion of thought insertion: The belief that someone is controlling your mind.

- Delusion of reference: The person falsely believes that insignificant remarks, events, or objects in one's environment have personal meaning or significance.

- Erotomania: A delusion in which someone falsely believes another person is in love with them.

- Grandiose religious delusion: The belief that the person is a god, or chosen to act as a god.

- Somatic delusion: A delusion about bodily functioning, bodily sensations, or physical appearance. Usually the false belief is that the body is somehow diseased, abnormal, or changed. A specific example is delusional parasitosis, where one feels infested with insects, bacteria, mites, spiders, lice, fleas, worms, or other organisms. Affected individuals may also report being repeatedly bitten. In some cases, entomologists are asked to investigate cases of mysterious bites. Sometimes physical manifestations may occur, including skin lesions.

- Delusion of poverty: The person strongly believes that he is financially incapacitated. Although less common now, it was particularly widespread in the days before state support. ("Delusion": http://en.wikipedia.org, accessed October 10, 2013.)

Neurotic Delusions

Neurosis refers to a category of mental disorders with characteristics of high levels of patient distress, but generally without the presence of delusions or hallucinations. For the neurotic, his behavior is generally within the bounds of "normal," socially acceptable limits, although this can be at the "outer fringes" at times. As with psychotic delusions, there are numerous kinds that may occur in neurosis, including obsessive-compulsive disorder, hypochondriasis, generalized anxiety disorder, conversion disorder, posttraumatic stress disorder, panic disorder, and countless varieties of phobias.

To the person afflicted, the effects can cause one or more negative mental states, including anxiety, anger, chronic irritability, mental confusion, low self-esteem, sadness, and chronic depression. This often leads to behavioral difficulties. Higher-level mental function can also be affected, leading to things such as cognitive problems like repetitive thought cycles, chronic daydreaming, and "magical thinking." The person's interpersonal relationships are always affected to some degree as well. Many times, his neurosis will leave him excessively dependent or aggressive, or fearful of social interaction. Some become perfectionists or carry with them totally inappropriate shame or guilt.

Common to all delusions is that they manifest in distorted thinking patterns. Some found in neurotic delusions are:

- All-or-none thinking: Looking at things in an "all-black" or "all-white" way.

- Overgeneralization: The individual views things and situations in extreme terms such as "it will never happen," "it always happens," "this is the end of the world," "I will never…," etc.

- Mental filter: The individual gets fixated on one or more negative thoughts.

- Discounting: The individual only looks at a negative aspect of something.

- Jump to conclusion: The individual makes a story in his head which may or may not be based on facts.

- Magnification or minimization: The individual blows things out of proportion or imagines them to be less important than they are.

- Emotional reasoning: The individual uses feelings to determine if something is true. For example, if I *feel* that you do not like me, I say you do not like me whether it is a fact or not.

- "Should" statements: The individual engages in extensive self-criticism.

- Blame: The individual takes responsibility for thoughts, feelings, and actions that may or may not have been within his or her control.

Importance of Treating Our Delusions

Neurotic delusions afflict a great number of people. I call them "delusions" because they are based on false beliefs that we build our world around. Often, delusions are a reaction to being uncomfortable and can include quick fixes that become potentially destructive. Recognizing that you have a "problem" and seeking the help necessary to deal with it is truly a life-changing step. Much of the time, we come to this place kicking and screaming after being threatened with divorce, job loss, jail time, or some other major life trauma. But the truth is that we knew deep down there was something wrong, even if we couldn't name it. Most of us have lived for years with the pain our condition has caused.

Chapter 2

Some Tools of the Trade

I have found two analytic tools that always seem to produce good results. One is called "birth order theory" and the other is the concept of "triangulation." These two concepts are critical to how people perceive themselves and the stress in their lives. It also explains how they eventually interact with others.

Birth Order Theory

Birth order, just like it sounds, refers to when you were born in relation to other siblings. Many noted psychologists believe that a person's birth order has a profound effect on personality development during his childhood that will last through his entire life. Alfred Adler (1870–1937), the Austrian psychiatrist who was a contemporary of Sigmund Freud and Carl Jung, was one of the first to say that birth order influences a person's personality, that it will influence how a person lives his life, deals with interpersonal relationships and with work, and handles virtually all activities we humans engage in.

Though the birth order theory has been challenged over the years, it still has many adherents. One of the most famous is Dr. Frank Salloway, Ph.D., whose book, *Born to Rebel*, claims that birth order has a huge impact on the "Big Five" personality traits of openness, conscientiousness, extraversion, agreeableness, and neuroticism..

Firstborn Children

Firstborn or only children tend toward work that gets them before the public in a big way. Some examples are Oprah Winfrey, Geraldo Rivera, Rush Limbaugh, and more than half of all U.S. presidents. They have natural leadership characteristics and generally are conscientious and reliable with perfectionist tendencies. Firstborns are generally aggressive, but are, at the same time, people-pleasers with a strong need for approval "from the top."

Only Children

Only children are firstborns on steroids. They exhibit even more perfectionist tendencies and are very conscientious; however, they get along better with older people than firstborns do.

Middle Children

Middle children have excellent people skills and can "read" people very well. They are also the peacemakers of the family and try to broker resolution between warring siblings. All these traits make them very independent and innovative. These are the entrepreneurs in the family. A middle child will feel as though the oldest gets all the attention while the youngest gets away with murder. Life doesn't seem very fair being caught in the middle. The middle child feels neglected and will keep to himself, and his thoughts and feelings will remain very much his own.

The middle child will often go outside the family to find attention, so his friends and peer groups become his family.

Last-Born Children

The "babies" of the family are usually the most social and extroverted. And they are the ones who always seem to be broke because they never had to learn to handle money: they got nearly everything they wanted from Mommy and Daddy, who spoiled them shamelessly. These are the "party animals" of the family and they love center stage. Jim Carrey, Steve Martin, and Billy Crystal are a few of the many famous youngest children in the entertainment industry. Though they are cute little devils, they have a tendency to be highly manipulative and very spoiled, and expect special treatment from those around them. This leads to friction among the other siblings, who are jealous of them.

*   *   *   *

But birth order is not the only factor that goes into the personality mix. The way the child's parents treat him is also a critical component. Because a firstborn doesn't come with an operating manual, his parents will experiment with what works and what doesn't. This will be a mix of "sage advice" from the grandparents, child-care books, discussions with peers, and so on. Generally, new parents will be more attentive and controlling with their first child. Rules will play a big role, and mothers especially will tend to be slightly neurotic in the "over-attention" department. Often this will lead to a child who becomes perfectionist and conscientious to a fault. Parental approval will be this child's major goal.

Having made their mistakes and honed their parenting skills on the firstborn, when the second child (the middle child if the parents go on to have another child) arrives, the parents have become somewhat "broken in" and are far more easygoing about their parenting. They no longer whisk their child off to the doctor at the first sign of fever or a cold. Now they must split their attention, which means that each child gets less. The second child knows nothing else, but it becomes a big adjustment for the firstborn child because he or she has had the limelight for so long. Life is easier for the second child since the parents have eased up. There is not the need to be the perfect little boy or girl, but he still has to compete for parental attention so will develop his people-pleasing skills to a far greater degree than the firstborn.

With less attention, the middle child shifts his focus outside the family, essentially looking for other avenues of attention attraction. Consequently, he generally has more friends and a wider peer group than either his older or younger siblings. He finds that he has quite a capability for getting people to like him. Also, since there is little reward at home from his parents, he is likely to be the family rebel, since "following the rules" at home doesn't elicit any attention. He is therefore very likely to take the opposite path from that of his older sibling.

The youngest child or last-born child grabs all of the parents' attention. He is the "apple of their eye." The parents are now very at ease with parenting and so afford the youngest pretty wide latitude. Finally, the parents can "sit back" and enjoy parenting. They have faced most of the inevitable child-rearing "crises" with their first two children, and now they just take things in stride. The pressure is off, so they can enjoy parenting the "baby" of the house. As a result, the last-born child is much less complicated and is freer than his other siblings. He is outgoing, a natural "people person," and enjoys life. On the dark side, he can also be manipulative and self-centered.

Though there are competing theories about what most influences a child's psychological development, birth order and the attendant parental response has significant impact. In my practice, I have seen enough to know the importance of birth order and how it shapes a person's personality. This is why birth order is one of the major markers I look for in working up every new client's case profile, and this tool has served me very well over the years.

Triangulation

Triangulation refers to the relationship dynamic where a member of a family (A) cannot, for whatever reason, communicate directly with another member of the family (B). Instead, what (A) does is enlist the help of another family member (C) to pass on a communication intended for (B). This occurs routinely in most families to one degree or another, but has harmful effects in dysfunctional families where it is used to a much greater degree.

Dr. Murray Bowen, M.D., was a prominent psychiatrist and researcher as well as one of the early pioneers in the family therapy and systemic therapy approaches to the diagnosis and treatment of psychological disorders affecting individuals and families. (Murray Bowen: *Family Therapy in Clinical Practice*. Lanham, MD: Jason Aronson Books, Rowman & Littlefield Publishers, Inc., 2004.) Dr. Bowen found that in dysfunctional families—those where conflict, neglect, or abuse are present and occur on a continual basis—there was a high level of triangulation. After studying this phenomenon over time, he concluded that it was a technique by which communication could be maintained between two family members who avoided direct dealings for any number of reasons. Inevitably, the A member would enlist the help of a C family member to carry messages to the B member. Bowen also found that triangulation occurred where, instead of message carrying, the C member was used as someone the A member could complain to about the B member.

An example would be a couple that gets separated or divorced and uses their child as the message carrier since they are not speaking with each other. Obviously, this places an enormous burden on the child, who may be damaged psychologically because he doesn't want to upset either parent. Triangulation is also commonly found in families where there is alcoholism or drug abuse or some other addictive or abusive behavior present. In these cases, the third family member, C, is generally used as the shoulder to cry on in the hope that he or she will be able to mediate the problem.

More often than not, it is the child in the family who falls into the C position. The child then feels forced to resolve the parents' problems by being a "perfect" child. This is especially true for daughters. Even though the family situation may be chaotic and unpredictable, the child feels that by being perfect she will be able to get the love of both parents. In some cases, the child will take the side of one parent because she needs the attention of the more nurturing parent, in most instances the mother. So the child will side with the mother and assist her in the ongoing war against the father. This is common in families where the father is, for instance, an active and abusive alcoholic or drug addict.

In triangulated families, the child begins to realize that he or she holds a tremendous amount of power and influence in the family. In the end, however, the child will inevitably begin to act out the parents' issues and will feel tremendous stress thinking that he or she must please both parents—an impossible task under these circumstances. The child is "damned if he does and damned if he doesn't."

It is rare to find any family where there isn't some triangulation going on. If the family has no major dysfunction happening, it is just a part of normal relationship interaction. When the family system is broken due to dysfunction, triangulation can become very harmful to the child involved. I see instances of wounded children in my practice all the time. They may now be grown up, but the scars last a lifetime. Also, the family roles we play out as a result of growing up in a dysfunctional family can impact how we develop family roles and learn these delusions. The most common of these family roles are enabler, hero, clown, scapegoat, and lost child.

These roles become defense mechanisms to fight off stress and discomfort. Enablers tend to try to control situations. Heroes tend to become judgmental and perfectionistic of themselves and others. The clown tends to minimize situations using humor and sarcasm. The scapegoat rebels to cover up feelings of shame and embarrassment. Finally, the lost child hides his feelings, which can become intense and lead to self-harm.

Chapter 3

My Story

When I was in my late twenties, I was married and raising children. I was also a bona fide workaholic. Much has changed since those days. My children are grown up with families of their own and I have been divorced and remarried and live on Mount Desert Island, Maine, where I continue my clinical practice. There is a clinical reason I am sharing my history with you. It illustrates how birth order and triangulation (family roles) worked in my family. I hope it allows you to take a look at your own life to see if you can identify any of these dynamics at work.

In the Beginning: Expression of Feelings

As a child, I can't remember my mother giving me a compliment or even being able to hug me, and it wasn't until my twenties that I wanted to hug her. There were a few reasons for this, but the big one for me was that I had become triangulated into my parents' relationship. This means that I was treated like a spouse and co-adult rather than as the child. My father would have discussions about his happiness and finances that he could/should have been having with my mother. My mother put expectations and responsibilities on me that she wasn't getting worked out with my father. My mother's feelings of abandonment had contributed to our distance, but her family of origin also may have contributed.

Her family was from the "old country." All her family lived in Italy. Although they were very expressive, they were not assertive with how they felt. My mother and her family were WW II survivors and were fascists. She was very black-and-white about her beliefs and had very poor communication skills due to the language barrier. After the war, my mother's family lost all their material possessions. She met my father in Europe and looked to him to be her knight in shining armor, which did not happen. After marrying my father and coming to the United States, she received no support from my father's family because his mother was emotionally dependent on him and resented my mother for taking him away. My mother then resorted to very negative thinking and was always looking at the world as a half-empty cup. She began to feel like a victim of her life.

When I was growing up, nobody in my family expressed negative feelings until someone "blew up." Most often it was my father whose fits of rage led to broken furniture and smashed walls, although he never hit us. With this dormant volcano ever present, I had difficulty expressing my feelings and needs. As a result, I held my feelings in and quietly seethed. I now remove myself to a quiet place until I can calm down, and once this is accomplished, I can discuss the matter at hand. Still to this day I must be very mindful of my reactions.

Family of Origin Atmosphere

My family atmosphere was moderately unpleasant, as there was constant tension and conflict. My role was that of the "parentified child." This meant that my needs were sacrificed so that I could fulfill the needs of my parents. As the rescuer, I was and still am involved in many family triangles. One key triangle was that involving myself, my father, and my paternal grandmother.

My paternal grandfather had died at age 49 of a heart attack, leaving my grandmother, my father and his sister feeling abandoned. My grandmother looked for my father to assume the provider role, which created a great deal of tension between my father, my mother, and my grandmother. The sudden death of my grandfather compounded my father's crises because of his family's immediately triangulating him back into his family of origin. My grandmother had lost her own mother at an early age: my great-grandmother had suffered many mental breakdowns that caused her to be away from home for years at a time. This had an enormous impact on my father's mother, leading to the unresolved dependency issues that affected her ability to parent her own son and daughter after her husband's death.

My father's life as a child was not an easy one even while his father was alive. His father thought of my father as "weak" and often told him so. He received very little nurturing from either his father or his mother. He had even been molested as a boy—and he was blamed for it while his mother made excuses for the molester. My father's family got developmentally stuck in the adolescent child stage (Duvall) and was unable to resolve boundary and power struggle issues that were further compounded by my grandfather's death and my father's marriage. (Evelyn Duvall: *Family Development*. New York: Lippincott, 1971.)

As a direct result, there was no room for new additions to my father's family, and my mother was therefore never accepted by them. The only way my mother was allowed into my father's family system was through my birth. Having a grandchild forced my grandmother to accept my mother if she wanted to see me, and I was triangulated between the two of them. My grandmother continued to try to have my father take on the provider role—which he relinquished—and then my grandmother turned to me, as young as age seven, to be her "helper."

As time passed, dyads occurred between my dad and I and my mom and sister. My sister, father, and mother had a triangle where my sister and mother would side against Dad. Because of her triangle with our parents and my triangle with them, my sister and I became pitted against each other or I was made to feel like her parent. My father left our family for two years when I was 12 and my sister was five. At this time, my sister struggled with fear of being abandoned and therefore became dependent on my mother. This is what led both my parents to view her as "needy" and me as "strong." I allowed them to relinquish their parental responsibility by becoming self-sufficient to a fault, while my sister demanded their attention and direction and continually experienced disappointment and ongoing feelings of abandonment. This put stress on the parental subsystem as well as on the family system as a whole.

A new triangle developed for me and my parents when I married in 1980. My own nuclear family and my parents were in the triangle. My ex-husband became the victim. My ex-husband depended heavily on me because of the lack of closeness he felt and his alienation in his own family of origin. This caused my mother to displace her hostility onto him. The triangle of my ex-husband, my father, and my mother allowed my parents to agree and be close while they jointly criticized and judged my ex-husband as a poor provider because he earned less than they felt was adequate. Also, a triangle consisting of myself, my ex-husband, and my mother existed where my mother and I joined forces against my ex-husband. I found this triangle destructive to my nuclear family. When I tried not to get triangulated, my mother became defensive and critical of me. At this point, our issues resurfaced—namely, that I always sided against her. It was the same when I was a child and used to side with my father.

My Nuclear Family—How I Got to Where I Am

My ex-husband and I have two daughters, and we are compatible according to the birth order theory. According to the theory, the older sibling of sisters (OSS) is dominant, assertive, and somewhat bossy. That was me. My ex-husband, according to the birth order theory, is the younger brother of a sister (YBS). In this scenario, the YBS has his sister in childhood cleaning up after him, etc. He is not a very regular worker, but is capable of great accomplishments provided there is a motherly figure around to take care of things. Ergo our major problem.

I met my ex-husband in New Jersey in 1979 and we married the next year. To escape the family triangulation, we moved to Florida in order to break away. However, after the birth of our oldest daughter, my family also moved to Florida. I became "re-triangled" due to financial and medical issues that arose for all of us. We believed that we could maintain our separateness but we failed. There was much warmth and tenderness between us except when money was concerned. Due to financial pressures, the door opened to allow my family once again to become triangled into our life. This caused my ex-husband and I to argue about finances often.

However, the real problem was that I could not "be all" or "do all," and my role as a mother suffered because I needed to be the breadwinner. That made me feel like I was repeating my own family history. I saw myself as the martyr and my ex-husband as nonsupportive financially. I tried to make up for my feelings of insecurity with work. This caused me to withdraw emotionally, and I began seeking the delusion of perfection to cover up my feelings of disappointment and frustration. As my resentments built, I started new triangles with my children. I bonded more with my older daughter because she was easy, made me feel adequate, and was the firstborn (OSS). I projected my feelings of frustration onto my youngest, the youngest sibling of a sister (YSS). I labeled her difficult instead of taking responsibility for my own feelings of distress.

Over time, my ex-husband and I could not overcome our breakdown in communication and the inability to unconditionally accept how we each thought, felt, and behaved. My ex-husband and I played out my parents' dramas, which led to my withdrawing emotionally and sexually. Our marriage ended. However, this event launched my personal journey to learn from my mistakes and to look at my role in what had caused my marriage to end.

Shortly after the divorce, I moved to Maine. Unfortunately, my younger daughter became triangled into her parents' issues and tried to quell her anxieties by developing control delusions. She today has taught herself how to do her best, self-soothe, shift her thinking, and be present versus being in control. As she will tell you, she is the "new and improved."

As a result of the divorce, my oldest daughter's delusion of perfection was challenged. Without the necessary tools, she turned to high-risk behaviors to self-medicate her disappointment and fear of change. After confronting her fears and fighting to resolve her anger, she has now become a respected educator and a parent who is still learning to assert her needs and balance her life and not repeat the "sins of her father and mother."

Both the girls have married and have beaten the "child from a divorced home" curse, which is the fear of commitment coupled with feelings of inadequacy. They work hard in their marriages to communicate, assert, and accept their thoughts, feelings, and actions. They strive not to fall into the bad habits that they saw in our family of origin. As far as birth order is concerned, my youngest, who is the last-born/only child, married an only child, and my oldest, the firstborn, married another firstborn. Godspeed to them both! They will need to learn to be comfortable with discomfort in order to accept themselves and their significant others. Because frustration and disappointment are normal, they no doubt will have delusions as a way to quick-fix feelings. They must respond and not react to their feelings so they can find contentment and true partnership. This is my hope and fervent wish.

My ex-husband and I have come to a place of acceptance. We have resurrected our friendship, each of us recognizing that we are and will always be our children's parents. We feel blessed for what we created together. The hurt, disillusionment, and resentments of the past have faded, and we both have been able to provide our children with a united front—and we act like a true "family." What does that mean? It means that as family members we give each other the space to be unique, and we accept how we each think, feel, and act even if we disagree at times. My ex and I have shared in each of our daughters' celebrations of high school and college graduations, birthdays, and weddings. We were both there as a family to welcome our first grandson into the world. Every holiday, we celebrate all together. For this I am grateful. We work together at giving our children the space to "launch" their own nuclear families, stepping aside with pride and satisfaction. Through it all, we did our job as parents.

Nuclear families offer us the opportunities to change and grow if we have the courage to honestly look at the patterns and learn from them.

*   *   *   *

After my first marriage ended, there was a period of chaos and confusion—just like during the 1998 ice storm in Maine or the 1992 hurricane named Andrew. The transition to Maine challenged us all. I even got involved with a person who I refer to as the "guide" to my reclaiming my soul. That relationship challenged me to use all my insights and to respond to the truths about myself and others. He was strong and stimulated me intellectually and sexually. He was also very destructive to me emotionally. I fought hard to stay in reality and not go into my perfection delusion: "going to make it work"—and after much turmoil, succeeded. Once that relationship ended and the dust settled, it was time to rebuild.

There was a lot of dust in the wind, but in the end, the soil settled, new seeds where planted, and the sprouts began to grow.

The goal for me at that time was to replace my reactionary world with a proactive environment. I made a transformation and began living "honestly." I filtered each and every action and reaction. I evaluated the feelings that had triggered the delusions I'd created, and, by filtering those feelings, prevented them from making me react. By doing this, I embraced the consequences of allowing the feelings to "just be" in my life, limited their reactions, and did not act out my fears. In other words, I now stop and ask myself, "Am I acting or *re*acting?" I came to realize that the only real choice I have in my life is that I must choose to be responsible and put in the work to live a truly proactive life, or continue living a *re*active life based on my own and other people's delusions. There has been no in-between. I began to find that as I practiced this new paradigm, my needs versus my wants became clearer, and I take responsibility for the choices I make in my life. By doing this on a consistent basis, I have found my true self.

* * * *

Then my current husband came into my life, two years after my divorce and move to Maine. At that point, I had decided to give up on relationships and focus on my daughters and getting to know my true self. The transition had been painful. My older daughter and I became estranged. My nuclear family felt abandoned because, as they put it, I had abdicated my role in the family. I set boundaries and limits both physically and emotionally. I got into a dark place and withdrew. During this time, I found love and lost it, got through the valley of fear, and faced my demons, ultimately learning to be comfortable with being uncomfortable. I challenged my perfection and control delusions and found peace and balance, which I now call my spirituality, in nature and life itself. I got back to basics and focused on simplicity. In honor of my new world view, I decided to retreat to the woods of northern Maine—and that's where I met my husband. There he was, as big as day, and he loves to tell the story as much as I do.

We had both gone to The Birches Resort on Moosehead Lake to get away. This is a beautiful and very quiet resort on the lake with multiple cabins in a pristine Maine countryside location. While there, we had a chance encounter in the dining room on Valentine's eve. The next morning, we once again accidentally met and this time shared a table over our cups of coffee. The rest is history.

He wasn't anything like the other men in my life. He was not an intellectual, but he was fun and exciting and physical—and 22 years my senior! He made me feel safe yet vulnerable at the same time. How is that possible? He was someone I could let my guard down with, someone who wanted to help me and contribute to my well-being. As I look back, I tore down the old house I was living in and laid the foundation for a new, more solid and durable home inside my heart. It seemed like he was sent by God to join me on this new journey.

During this time, my father was diagnosed with lung cancer and he only got to meet my husband once before he died. Sadly, on the eve of our wedding, my father lapsed into a coma. My husband took care of everything and got me and my girls back to Florida to be with my dad during his last days. We were married on April 9, 2000, and Dad died on April 13th.

Today my husband and I live on Mount Desert Island, Maine. Our home stands in the middle of Acadia National Park and is one of the most peaceful, spiritual places on this earth. It is a place that supports my need for simplicity. We have been married now for almost 14 years. We are committed to not repeating the mistakes we made in our past relationships and to working hard at communicating by responding instead of reacting to each other. We work at unconditionally accepting how we each think, feel, and act. We strive to feel *with* each other instead of *for* each other. What I mean by this is that we each try not to judge or fix the other's feelings, but just accept them and walk each other through whatever feelings we are experiencing. These are not easy tasks for two very strong-willed alpha personalities. We accept that our marriage is a work in progress. Marriage is an adult's way to attach, which allows companionship that provides the security that allows for work and exploration. That is our goal. My husband is the YBS and I am the OSS. Great, right?

What I do and how I do it

I have been asked many times over the years why I became a therapist. The answer to this is multitiered. I knew from a very early age that I wanted to help people. A guidance counselor noticed that I was the one all the other kids confided in. He took me aside one day and told me that I had a natural way of listening and really hearing what others were saying. He then suggested I consider college to study social work, which in the '70s was a new major that had evolved out of the social sciences/sociology areas of study. He helped me pick schools and get scholarships and here I am.

Work history, early training, and current practice areas

I have been practicing social work from the perspective of a trained psychotherapist for 38 years and I still love it. I have been involved in some very exciting, cutting-edge treatments that are closely correlated to brain science and its impact on mental health and behaviors. Neurofeedback, a treatment method that has been in use for over 20 years, is one of the treatment methods I use. It was born from the field of biofeedback and is also called EEG biofeedback. It is, at its core, a brain exercise where the clinician observes the brain in action from moment to moment by monitoring its brainwaves. The clinician shows the brain activity to the patient and then, utilizing the skill of "mindfulness," through the use of images, sounds, and tactile responses, the client learns to reward and reinforce positive shifts in his or her own brain states. Neurofeedback (NFB) is mind training through self-regulation. Good self-regulation is necessary for optimal brain function. Self-regulation training enhances the function of the central nervous system and thereby improves mental performance, emotional control, and physiological stability. NFB is like putting someone's brain on a stair-stepper to continuously exercise certain regulatory functions.

Cognitive Behavioral Therapy, otherwise known as CBT, has been a mode of treatment I have developed expertise in since the 1980s, when I was an addiction counselor in a teen rehab center in South Florida. The evolution of CBT for me started with becoming skilled in *reality therapy*. Developed by Dr. William Glasser in the 1960s, reality therapy is grounded in the principles of choice therapy. As time went on, I began to branch out and started using Rational Emotive Therapy (RET), which is a psychotherapeutic approach that proposes that unrealistic and irrational beliefs cause many emotional problems. From the foundations of this approach evolved another approach referred to as Rational Emotive Behavior Therapy (REBT) founded by Albert Ellis, an approach I have embraced clinically and which has proven to be most effective. This approach evolved into what we refer to now as a category of therapeutic techniques collectively known as cognitive behavioral therapy.

The work of Dr. David Burns (1980s), Dr. Edward S. Friedman (1990s), and Daniel Amen (2000s) fine-tuned CBT for me. I now use CBT with NFB and other complementary approaches. This multifaceted treatment modality is action-oriented, and I have found that patients progress quicker when they are actively engaged in the treatment experience. In simple terms, CBT starts where the client is now and helps him or her focus on how their past triggers reactions in their current lives. CBT gives the client the tools to *respond* instead of *react* to their life experiences. Putting both CBT and NFB together as a treatment package has been very exciting and powerful. Neurofeedback is not yet widely taught in medical schools or psychology/social work graduate programs, so many psychotherapy professionals are unaware of the efficacy of this technique.

In 2009, I began incorporating the use of video games, music, and brain exercises to enhance the treatment of my patients who were struggling with issues of anxiety, attention deficit disorder, and depression. A colleague of mine became aware of my use of these techniques and informed me about NFB, thinking that I would find it complementary to my practice. As a result, I contacted Dr. Siegfried Othmer in California, who, together with his wife Susan (B.A. /B.C.I.A.C.), has been developing the foremost instrumentation for neurofeedback. They also founded the EEG Institute, which provides clinical services to the therapeutic community (learn more at www.eeginfo.com). I took an introduction course and was very impressed with how our brain regulates our thoughts, emotions, and behaviors. I have learned that by improving brain function, we assist clients in improving how they function cognitively, emotionally, and behaviorally. This complements the talk therapy process. Using this combination of therapies, I have found that my clients achieve their treatment goals more quickly and efficiently, and that the changes they make are more long-lasting and, in some cases, permanent.

Since 2009, the implementation of neurofeedback has taken major leaps and bounds. In 2013, I completed my national certification process. The American Academy of Pediatrics has placed NFB as a level one "best support" for ADHD (attention deficit hyperactivity disorder). The National Institutes of Health lists more than 8,500 peer-reviewed publications on biofeedback, 450 on neurofeedback, and 130,000 scientific publications on EEG.

In 2012, the Othmers spearheaded Homecoming for Veterans (HC4V). This is a national outreach program dedicated to providing free NFB treatment for military veterans and active-duty service members suffering from posttraumatic stress disorder (PTSD), traumatic brain injury (TBI), and substance abuse. For more info on HC4V go to www. hc4v.org. I am proud to say I am part of this program.

Overall, my cornerstone as a professional is that I strive to practice what I preach and I live my life with intent. I attempt to prevent stagnation and becoming compliant.

Chapter 4

The Perfection Delusion

People with the perfection delusion have an internal motivation to constantly strive to be perfect in everything they do. Many high achievers have strong perfectionist instincts but would not necessarily be considered neurotic or maladaptive since they don't invest their entire sense of self-worth in the outcome. If they fail to reach their goal, though disappointed, they will not go into a tailspin of depression. In fact, many high-achieving artists, scientists, and athletes, among other fields, turn out to be the famous people of history. Their work ethic and tireless attention to the details of their professions exceed those of their peers and sets them apart. They become the heroes of their industries and models to be emulated. Intense focus and unrelenting attention to detail lead them to success, and in many cases, fame. These people have been referred to as "adaptive" perfectionists. This is considered a positive personality trait. They will continually strive for excellence and are always conscientious and meticulous. They have high self-esteem and a low level of self-criticism.

On the other hand, the person with the perfection delusion will not accept anything less than what he considers absolute perfection. When he fails to achieve this self-imposed goal, depression follows. For this individual, his entire self-worth is based on reaching an unrealistic standard. Unlike the high achiever who takes pleasure in pursuing his task, the delusional perfectionist will dread every step in the process because he believes that he will never be able to complete the task in a manner that meets his unrealistic expectations. Psychologists refer to this personality type as "maladaptive." (D. E. Hamachek: "Psychodynamics of

Normal and Neurotic Perfectionism" in *Psychology*, 15: 27–33.)

For women, perfectionism is often seen in obsessive attention to their physical attractiveness. Their looks become a central focus of their lives. With the current state of media projecting countless images of attractive and therefore "desirable" women in movies, TV, magazines, etc., women—and especially young girls—internalize the overriding cultural message that unless they are physically attractive they have little worth. Though it is well known that most of this messaging is driven by the advertising industry trying to sell beauty products and clothing, the impact is profound on these women and on our culture as well. Since in these instances perfectionism attaches value to what the society and culture deem valuable, many women feel compelled to look as thin and well-dressed as possible. Often they are fighting against their individual body types in the vicious pursuit of needing to "look good."

The "perfect" woman in our society is also supposed to be professionally accomplished, married, and a mother. Unless she has the complete culturally prescribed "package," she is a loser. If a woman has a career, it will take time away from her children and household. If she focuses too much on her children and home life, she will not be able to compete in the business world. On top of all that, she must be thin, well-coiffed, and well-dressed at all times. The "inner critic" for these women is working overtime telling them they aren't thin enough and aren't good enough mothers, wives, homemakers, etc. It is no wonder that today's woman finds herself caught in a no-win cultural trap.

Behavior problems

The delusional perfectionist is prone to developing behavior problems due to his or her defective and toxic beliefs, and one of the most common behavior problems is procrastination. Since everything must be perfect and the perfectionist knows how hard it is to reach that goal, he will frequently put off starting the task. By contrast, the high achiever will take the task in stride and commence his or her methodical and painstakingly meticulous work. Meanwhile, the delusional perfectionist will suffer from a high level of stress and anxiety because he knows the works must get done at some point. This may lead to depression and intense irritability that makes it very unpleasant to be around him. Consequently, interpersonal relationships are often damaged, sometimes to the point of no return, leading to separation, divorce, or estrangement.

In other cases, the discomfort caused by this delusion may turn the person toward self-medication. This can take the form of drug or alcohol abuse, which only serves to intensify the perfectionist's already low sense of self-worth. If the substance abuse becomes chronic, the usual consequences will follow: loss of job, spouse, and children, financial problems, other addictions, and so on.

For women who have as part of their delusional package the cultural beauty image, eating disorders are very common. These dangerous behaviors help the perfectionist to cope with the stress and anxiety produced by fear of failure to live up to their own unrealistic standards. Eating disorders are often the only way that person knows to relieve, if only momentarily, the horrible discomfort they suffer.

Anorexia nervosa is a condition often found in perfectionist women, particularly younger women. The main characteristic of this condition is the person's refusal to maintain a healthy body weight. Frequently, women will turn to excessive exercising, extremely restrictive diets, and/ or abuse of laxatives, diuretics, or diet pills, singly or in some combination that they have found works for them to lose body weight. These individuals are terrified of even the slightest weight gain. Anorexia is a very serious condition that leads to death if left untreated.

Purging is another eating disorder that can occur in perfectionist women. These individuals try to maintain or lose body weight by repeatedly purging themselves. This takes the form of self-induced vomiting immediately after a meal. This action produces temporary relief from the feeling of fullness and fear of putting on weight. But it is *only* temporary relief, so the cycle must be repeated after every meal. As with anorexia, this is a serious problem that leads to severe medical problems and requires prompt treatment.

Bulimia nervosa is a kind of combination of purging disorder and binging disorder. In this condition, the bulimic gets caught up in a binge/ purge cycle where she eats a large amount of food in a very short period of time. This is usually done in private. Purging soon follows, generally through self-induced vomiting. The bulimic is just as obsessed with weight gain and body image as the anorexic, and, like the anorexic, if left untreated, the bulimic will die from this disorder.

Case history

She presented a striking appearance on first glance, and after we established a rapport, I could see the pain in her face, reflecting the (largely self-induced) suffering she had endured for most of her life. Serafina reported a history of depression, anxiety, and PTSD.

The seeds were planted by early abuse and neglect by her parents, which was only exacerbated when a childhood medical condition prohibited her parents from visiting her in the hospital. This compounded her already developed sense of worthlessness in the eyes of those on whom she depended for love and support above all others.

To cover her intense pain, in her own clearly underdeveloped emotional manner, she began very early in adolescence to seek "love" wherever she could find it, acting out sexually (throwing an abortion into the mix), and abused substances to try to quell her ever-increasing emotional pain. Despite her futile attempts to "cure" or at least medicate her often unbearable mind-set (i.e., black/white, good girl/bad girl thinking), nothing seemed to really help. Utterly convinced that her feelings simply didn't matter anyway, she began to shut them out completely, which, in her mind, was her only path to "safety."

Recent years had brought with them the diagnosis of Lyme disease, which sent her into a total tailspin and resurrected the PTSD syndrome she had suffered as a young child—but this time on steroids—and amplified in her mind the feelings of "lost child" abandonment. Clearly, to find her way "home" to the authentic self she never even knew existed, our sessions had to begin with a guided approach to having her challenge her automatic knee-jerk reactions (i.e., the coping skills she had carefully honed over the years for dealing with extreme or unexpected stress…her way of intellectualizing her feelings). Rather, through our time together, Serafina slowly learned instead how to *acknowledge* these feelings in order to begin the all-important journey toward physical and emotional freedom, the true components of ultimate emancipation.

As perfectionism was clearly the underlying cause of her delusions, utilizing yoga and meditation proved to be most useful in terms of allowing her to sit with her emotions rather than judging them or attempting to quick-fix them "away" by making others happy.

Today, this young lady (at least at heart and in spirit) is at peace and seems to have found her true calling, from which she derives great *personal* satisfaction.

Not only is she working with other women, but she is vigorously pursuing her artistic talent. Her mind-set about being "good" only when caring for others and "bad" when caring for herself was repeatedly challenged, and ultimately the monumental importance of self-care was seriously addressed and absorbed. I'm very happy and gratified to report that Serafina is now able to set boundaries for herself and with others by expressing what she needs and feels. I firmly believe that because of the often difficult and challenging work we accomplished together, she is on the path to a wonderful, fulfilling, and happy life. Where once stood a young woman incarcerated in a hell of her own making now stands a vibrant, confident, inspiring woman who is totally free to venture wherever her heart leads her!

Treatment

After obtaining a history and a review of the client's reason for referral—i.e., why they are here and what they want to change—we begin the *process* of change. We discuss their strengths and weaknesses, develop a genogram, which is similar to a family tree, identify communication patterns learned from their past, and then set goals that will get them out of the delusion they have created. The treatment plan is then written up and, as a team, we develop new skills that get us to the completion of treatment and free from the discomfort.

Utilizing CBT logs, recommending yoga and meditation, and referring the patient to various self-help tools such as Louise Hayes's work are some of the therapeutic tools used. In the accompanying illustrations, you can see the kinds of goals and objectives that we set.

Stress Management tx plan

Client Name:_____ Date: _____

Problem: Stress Management – feels overwhelmed by too many responsibilities and has difficulty balancing efficient productivity and self-care

Long Term Goal: Feels that personal responsibilities/commitments are manageable and reports increased balance between various facets of their life

Short Term Goal (STG):

   1. Time management   **Target Date:** _____

   2. Increased self-care in the form of involvement in leisure activities, allowance of some unstructured time daily, and consistency in practicing other actions that support basic physical and mental health (i.e. sufficient sleep, proper nutrition, exercise, etc.)   **Target Date:** _____

   3. Client will practice realistic self-talk to reduce the negative effects of self-defeating or distorted thinking on their stress level   **Target Date:** _____

   4. _____   **Target Date:** _____

Procedures/Methods

   STG 1: Client will review in session daily schedule of activities and receive assistance in prioritizing demands, streamlining daily routines, reducing procrastination, and improving overall organization

   STG 2: The client and therapist will explore the importance of self-care and identify how to incorporate it into their daily routine. Assertiveness skill-building will also be incorporated if "saying no" to unnecessary commitments is difficult. Additionally, the client will receive help in developing and utilizing a support system identifying social supports to help them engage in regular self-care.

   STG 3: The client will identify distorted thinking patterns such as perfectionism, or believing that they must do everything themselves, that contribute to daily stress. The client will identify positive affirmations and realistic self-talk scripts to repeat to themselves to challenge the distorted thinking.

Indicators

   STG 1: Client will report a more efficient, productive daily routine

   STG 2: Client reports increased self-care

   STG 3: Client expresses thoughts that support stress management

   STG 4: _____

Client Signature: _____

Counselor Signature: _____

Complex PTSD tx plan

Client Name: _____ Date: _____

Problem 1: Ongoing Work on Resolving Complex PTSD Issues

Long Term Goal: To learn to safely recognize, express and manage the defensive coping strategy of anger generated in response to memoires from childhood trauma/neglect and ongoing disappointment related to parental lack of concern and involvement with client's family of procreation.

Short Term Goal 1: Allow client to identify and express pent-up feelings related to disappointment over childhood abuse and trauma and to understand the resulting connections with current behaviors.
                                                    Target Date:

Short Term Goal 2: Cultivate a change of coping strategy from use of the maladaptive coping defense of excessive anger for self-protection to an alternative behavior more adaptive for interactions in her current adult role.   **Target Date:**

Short Term Goal 3: Reinforce with client her own sense of self-esteem and self-confidence as she reviews her trauma history in the light of the positive perspective of all she has learned from it and how it has facilitated her own growth and increased her compassion for others. **Target Date:**

Procedures/Methods:
   STG 1: Client will verbalize in session and journal at home regarding feelings stimulated by recognition of family of origin's empathic failures in childhood and accept supportive feedback validating these reactions.
   STG 2: Work through in sessions the feelings underlying client's surface reaction of excessive anger to recognize and then have some choice about changing maladaptive defensive behaviors to more mature and less alienating ways of coping.
   STG 3: Explore with client use of the book titled *A Gift to Myself* by Charles L Whitefield, MD to further strengthen her sense of self-efficacy.
Measurable Indicators:
   STG 1: Remaining faithful to every other week therapy sessions and sharing verbally plus through journaling between sessions at home about feelings.
   STG 2: Continue to fill out the worksheets provided by the counselor.
   STG 3: Facilitate client's generation of a list of strengths and blessings in reviewing her life thus far and establish a set of goals for further personal growth.

Client Signature:_____

Counselor Signature: _____

Chapter 5

The Control Delusion

People affected by what I refer to as the control delusion come in two main types. The first are the people who have an inordinate need to make sure they have control over as many aspects of their lives as possible, from their daily schedule to their diet, wardrobe, choice of friends, home environment, aspects of their work, and so on. What sets them apart from what we would otherwise merely think of as people who are highly organized is that they become very anxious if things become disrupted in any of these highly organized areas of their lives. For example, if there is a major change in their daily work schedule that they had no control over, or if they are asked to take on a new and unfamiliar task at work, this can cause a high level of stress and even depression.

Granted, this would cause most people to become somewhat stressed, but the difference is one of degree. For the "control" person, the stress level is highly elevated, starts to affect their performance, and may cause reactive behaviors such as lashing out at coworkers or family members. Only after some time has passed do they adjust to the new circumstances with a semblance of regained control.

Then there are those who feel the overwhelming need to control the actions and lives of those around them. We have all encountered these people. They are the ones who are always on hand to offer mostly unwanted and unsolicited advice. They are also the ones who, because of their subconscious power needs, need to be "in charge" and get their way.

In addition to these two principal types is what I call the "blended" type who needs to control not only their environment, but other people, as well.

The control delusion exhibits itself somewhat differently in men and women. For instance, men tend to manifest these issues by controlling others either at home or at work as a way to coping with their subconscious fears and insecurities. Some men exhibit their control issues by being abusive, which can take the form of verbal, physical, mental/ emotional, or sexual abuse. In any case where this is found, the abuse is used as a way to inflict pain on the victims because the abusers are in an extraordinary amount of pain themselves even though they may not consciously recognize it.

In our society, it is seen as important for a man to be "powerful." If a man feels "weak" or vulnerable, this can affect his self-image to a profound degree. In instances like this, it is common for such men to try to regain their sense of power (and thus their sense of masculinity) by controlling those around them. For this type of man, the safest people to do this with are members of his immediate family, in particular his wife and children. Even though these men hide their emotional pain pretty well, even from themselves, on some level they are usually aware of it and will feel the need to exercise control over their family members by making them suffer through some form of abuse in an attempt to transfer their own pain onto someone else—someone they believe will pose little threat of retaliation.

In other cases that are not outright abusive, men will attempt to control their partners by forbidding them to associate with various people or groups. Members of that person's family or their friends are often targets for this. Some men will dictate what foods the family members can eat, what religion they can observe, what types of clothing they can wear, what books they can read, etc. This type of behavior is controlling and may occur on a greater or lesser scale, but it provides the man with the "power" that he sees as missing in some other important part of his life, generally at work.

Unlike men, women tend to exhibit control over various *things* in their lives as a way to feel empowered. Though they may also try to exert control over people, particularly their children, much of the time their control issues deal with things like food, body image, guilt, anxiety, self-harm, or addictions as a way out of the pain caused by an exaggerated sense of loss of control. This is particularly true of women who were victims themselves, generally in their childhoods. These women are highly likely to become abusive to others in their misguided effort to regain a sense of control in their own lives. Abandonment, neglect, addiction, and physical, sexual, or mental abuse cause women intense emotional pain that may cause them to turn outward to find the things they can control in an effort to ease their suffering. The path to mental health in some ways is easier for women because they do not have the "masculinity" burden that men carry and are more open to seeking treatment.

Behavior problems

As mentioned above, the control delusion can result in a diverse set of negative behaviors, some of which are more prevalent with men and some with women. With men, many times these behaviors take some form of abuse, usually within the family setting with the wife and children the victims. For men, control issues outside the family normally take place at work, where the individual will attempt to control his coworkers and others with whom he comes in contact and who he views as nonthreatening.

For women, controlling behaviors involving other people will largely revolve around family members, mostly her children, to whom she will give unsolicited advice even after they're grown. If they are still living at home and are under her care, she will tend to micromanage their daily affairs to a greater or lesser degree depending on the level of the severity of her delusion.

Interpersonal problems

Much depends on the degree of the controlling behaviors involved and their nature. In highly abusive circumstances, such as physical abuse of the spouse or children, court intercession is often called for, with court-ordered restraint of visitation and mandated treatment. In less traumatic cases where the controlling behavior is somewhat more benign, partial or full estrangement may occur. It goes without saying that, left unchecked, the person with control issues will ultimately alienate those around him or her, which will, of course, increase the person's unhappiness and suffering.

Case history

As a therapist, and more importantly, as a mother and now a grand-mother, it is nearly impossible for me to witness, without wincing, an individual who, although now an adult, is so severely hobbled by the emotional shackles resulting from the unresolved pain of his past, he has simply ceased to thrive, develop, and ultimately grow.

Such was the case with Sam, a fifty-year-old white male with a history of chronic pain he had borne, virtually alone, since childhood. Born into a family where toughing it out, regardless of the problem (emotional or physical), was expected, Sam's seeds of delusion, particularly with regard to control, were planted and cultivated practically from his first breath. In the deeply dysfunctional and utterly detached-from-reality climate in which he was raised—where necessary and healthy coping skills are supposed to be taught—what Sam learned was that, "If you are in pain, you are not in control; hence you are weak and inadequate." This sort of black-and-white thinking, served up in multiple helpings of reinforcement each day, in the end only serves to reinforce feelings of hopelessness in a child (or anyone, for that matter, who doesn't have the self-assurance to reject such subliminal and destructive directions, particularly when the "messenger" is most frequently the parent or some other figure of authority who the person loves, respects, and wants desperately to please). Inevitably, the resulting manifestation of such indoctrination is a series of panic attacks (potentially lasting a lifetime) if the issue goes unresolved.

Once launched, the original delusion starts to have "puppies," very often leading to chronic depression that ignites a downward emotional spiral. In some cases, if left untreated, this can, in turn, lead to the suffering person's ultimate demise, when the pain of life and the realization that one can control nothing but him actually becomes a reality. The depression is attached to disappointment (for various and often many reasons), and this disappointment "lifts the veil" just long enough to reveal to the sufferer that it, too, is attached to something—usually deep-seated physical and/or emotional pain that triggers thoughts and feelings of deep inadequacy. In the end, this leaves the sufferer with overwhelming feelings of unsureness and a lack of self-confidence.

This ongoing cycle of absolute despair continues throughout the lifetime of the tortured patient, and one day, their inability to exist in a world full of such intense discomfort either drives them to therapy or, sadly and all too often, to mental breakdown or suicide.

However, in my professional experience, I have found that using CBT logs to identify the automatic delusions, enabling the patient to become aware of their emotional and intellectual reaction to painful and uncomfortable situations, and employing tools such as music and positive affirmations can significantly help them in differentiating disappointment from physical discomfort.

Once that milestone has been reached, the patient's ability to stop the automatic reaction to physical pain, something that is out of his or her control and hence, hopeless, can be turned around into something that can be viewed as manageable. By staying in the moment and taking "baby steps" toward the goal of increased tolerance of discomfort, all the while repeating the mantra (as often as necessary), "I can handle anything in this moment because I now realize it won't last forever," helps redirect one's thoughts toward the ultimate goal of greater self-esteem and belief in one's innate capabilities to cope with any situation that arises.

As a wonderful result, with diligent practice and dedication, the individual eventually emerges as one whom, unlike in the past, is now able to complete tasks, set future goals, and increase his or her feeling of adequacy. Cumulatively, this results in a marked decrease in depression, thus freeing the individual to pursue a happy, relatively emotionally unencumbered life.

Treatment

After obtaining a history and a review of the client's reason for referral—i.e., why they are here and what they want to change—we begin the *process* of change. We discuss their strengths and weaknesses, develop a genogram, which is similar to a family tree, identify communication patterns learned from their past, and then set goals that will get them out of the delusion they have created. The treatment plan is then written up and, as a team, we develop new skills that get us to the completion of treatment and free from the discomfort.

Utilizing CBT logs, recommending yoga and meditation, and refer-ring the patient to various self-help tools such as Louise Hayes's work are some of the therapeutic tools used.

CBT with guided imagery and suggested reading were also utilized in the treatment process. The feeling logs help identify the distortions from reality. In the accompanying illustrations, you see a sample treat-ment plan used as a roadmap for the treatment process.

Adjustment Disorder tx plan

Client Name _____ Date: _____

Problem 1: Adjustment Disorder issues pertaining to the following identifiable stressor and causing the following emotional, behavioral, and social symptoms –

_____

Long Term Goal: To alleviate the distress triggered by the above event and improve general coping

Short Term Goals (STG)

1. To vent thoughts and feelings associated with the change or loss and receive supportive feedback   **Target Date:**_____
2. To identify and counter negative self-talk that exacerbates the maladaptive reaction to the above stressor   **Target Date:** _____
3. To develop healthy coping strategies and identify alternative ways of managing and resolving issues   **Target Date:**_____
4. Boost self-confidence and optimism by identifying personals assets/strengths and external resources for healing   **Target Date:**_____
5. _____**Target Date:** _____

Procedure/Methods:

STG 1: Exploration of thoughts and feelings in sessions and journal writing or "homework assignments" in between sessions

STG 2: Therapist will introduce the concept of "self-talk" and help to identify maladaptive thinking patterns and positive counter statements/affirmations

STG 3: Therapist will assist the client in identifying (verbally and on paper) ideas for self-care and positive management of symptoms and help them rearrange their daily schedules to allow for the practice of these positive coping strategies

STG 4: The client will identify (verbally and on paper) inner and external resources for healing and will review in sessions methods for successful coping in past life transitions

STG 5: _____

Measurable Indicators:

STG 1: The client regularly attends therapy sessions, verbalizes the impact of the event on their life and mood, and is receptive to supportive feedback

STG 2: Process in therapy and self-report of increased awareness of the impact of thinking patterns on their behavior and mood.

STG 3: The client self-reports the ability to use alternative coping skills in real life situations

STG 4: Process in therapy and self-report of being able to draw on existing strengths to adjust to the change and loss

Client Signature:_____ Counselor Signature: _____

Chapter 6

The Guilt Delusion

Guilt is the regret we feel when we act in a way that is contrary to our internal moral code or conscience. Guilt is a healthy emotion when it is grounded in reality; it serves to tell us what is "wrong" and to keep us from doing bad things. Without healthy guilt, civilization as we know it could not survive. We would instead live in a world governed by the "law of the jungle," with the strong taking from the weak in an "everyone for themselves" free-for-all. Healthy guilt is an appropriate response to doing bad things like harming others. The pain the guilty conscience produces in the emotionally healthy individual is usually enough to keep most people behaving in a civilized manner. If they have done something wrong, they learn that the surest way to alleviate their guilt is through atonement by making amends, apologizing, or accepting punishment.

Guilt becomes neurotic when it bears little relationship to the reality of the cause. Neurotic guilt involves a chronic feeling of responsibility for the pain or suffering of others, which may or may not have been caused by the "guilty" individual, and this pain cannot be eliminated even through efforts made to atone for the perceived wrong. Another way of distinguishing between healthy guilt and neurotic guilt is to say that healthy guilt motivates a person to behave in the best manner to serve not only his or her best interests, but those of the other people involved. The individual will promptly try to right any wrong. Neurotic guilt exists where the individual, whether amends are made or not, cannot shake the pain associated with the wrongdoing. In some cases, the wrongdoing is merely imagined. Neurotic guilt inhibits the individual's natural expression of self and makes it difficult for him or her to form intimate bonds with others. It has a lasting negative effect on self-esteem.

The origins of guilt are normally found in childhood. As very young children, we have no sense of right and wrong behavior. That is something imposed upon us by our parents and caregivers from the earliest age. As we get a bit older, institutions outside our families, such as our churches and schools, impose additional codes of acceptable behavior on our still impressionable psyches. Some parents and early childhood environments are stricter than others, adhering to dogmatic moral codes usually based on their religious affiliations, and many households maintain these very strict rules of behavior for their children. Consequently, children raised in these environments will carry with them (generally for the rest of their lives) a very rigid internal code of acceptable behavior.

Another source of heightened internal moral code comes from being raised in families that require their children to be overly responsible. These families inculcate this value system (perfectionism) in their children by harshly criticizing or faulting them when they don't live up to the standards set by the parents. Children from such families develop a sense of "super responsibility." In some cases, this can be an asset that leads to conscientious task-tending. However, the downside is that it generally makes the individual extremely sensitive to criticism from authority figures like employers and teachers. For these individuals, criticism will lead to a sharp drop in self-esteem and feelings of self-worth since so much of their sense of self is wrapped up in meeting the expectations of authority figures. They will develop an "inner critic" to protect themselves from external criticism, and this inner critic will make sure that their behavior not only meets but exceeds that which they perceive as expected.

Unlike many other "delusions," normal guilt can be dealt with fairly easily by taking atonement measures like apologizing, making amends for damage done through restitution, and so on. These are direct actions that will alleviate the person's guilt feelings to a significant degree. Neurotic guilt has no such escape hatch.

Neurotic guilt generally involves feelings of responsibility for things that the person had no control over or maybe even no involvement with. The classic example is "survivor guilt," where a person feels guilty that he or she survived some traumatic event when others did not. However, much more common is neurotic guilt resulting from the individual's belief that he or she has not lived up to an excessively high standard internalized from early childhood. Overly harsh models of acceptable behavior result in individuals who magnify mistakes or offenses they believe they have made out of proportion to reality.

Behavior Problems

Neurotic guilt will lead the individual to any one or more negative behaviors in his attempt to avoid or reduce the pain he suffers. Such behaviors increase the likelihood that the person will exhibit one or more of the following traits:

- Low self-esteem
- Depression
- Weight issues due to overeating
- Chronic anxiety
- Compulsive behaviors—drug or alcohol abuse, gambling, getting into debt, etc.
- Obsessional thoughts
- Relationship issues with spouse, children, family, coworkers, and others
- Taking responsibility for everything that goes wrong
- Becoming a people-pleaser
- Becoming a peacekeeper
- Trying to make everyone happy

Case history

Any baby born to an active alcoholic or any other addicted parent (particularly the mother) should have "Guilt Delusion" stamped on their birth certificate right next to his or her footprints, for the certainty of that trait revealing itself as the child grows will be just as identifiable. It's a given that all children seek, as the first thing in life, the approval of their parents. It is (and unfortunately, can become) an all-consuming goal when it is not appropriately achieved. But the rules of the game change drastically for the child of an alcoholic/addict, who finds that so passionately desired "brass ring" is just always just out of reach. Hence, the child takes on the responsibility of "fixing" the problem that is keeping him from reaching this most elusory but necessary goal.

Clearly ill-equipped to handle a problem that has baffled the best medical minds for centuries, when the patient/parent is not willing or able to seek the kind of professional help necessary, the child's inability to achieve such a monumental task—an almost impossible feat—is internalized as a failure on his part, and that is when the ever-increasing and unbearably painful delusion of guilt sets in. But that first failed attempt to fix the wrongs and make things right sets off a chain of unfortunate events as the child continues to grow and his and her circle widens. Accordingly, these events fuel the fire of the guilt that ultimately comes to serve as the core of the way he or she perceives him- or herself. Everything that goes wrong in this person's life and in the lives of those who surround him—anything that he can't personally rectify—adds another brick to the wall of guilt that ultimately engulfs him. In the end, guilt has won and reigns supreme; inevitably, with all the anger about his perceived "failures" turned inward, the result is acute depression. The lucky few who have the last gasp of energy to seek help often come to understand the root of their problems. Unfortunately, most go on to live lives of quiet despair. Thankfully, Gia fell into the former category, and when she walked into my office for the first time, the self-inflicted suffering she had endured for decades was boldly etched on her sad face.

The child of an alcoholic, she like most so born, craved the attention she had never received from the start. In an effort to "stuff" her feelings and self-medicate, she was a compulsive overeater, the results of which (being severely overweight) only served to compound and verify to her that, in truth, she was "not good enough." To cope, she became a consummate people-pleaser, which ignited the delusion that "if I make people happy, I feel all right, for I feel very guilty if people are mad at me." Any sort of negative feedback in any realm ignited tremendous fear in her. However, when guilt is based on taking responsibility for others' actions, one becomes completely unable to set any sort of boundaries, thus compounding the problem. The anger she feels toward others for disappointing her, and her perceived failure to "fix" the problems, are turned inward and become guilt.

As contradictory as it may seem from a logical perspective, because she takes personal responsibility for others, guilt helps her avoid taking responsibility for herself. Guilt deludes and aids in the avoidance of her own deep-seated emotional pain. It enables her to avoid feeling rejected and masks the true core of her distress. The end result is that guilt helps her to avoid asserting her needs. The delusion is, "If I take responsibility for others, then I can have a false sense of control, which serves to protect me against the unbearable pain that constantly rages inside me."

Sadly, the very opposite occurs, as Gia's pain from disappointment gets internalized and leaves her unfulfilled and emotionally alone. However, with the help of CBT logs, she is learning to challenge her feelings of guilt and stay in the moment with the pain and disappointment. In so doing, she is learning to evaluate what *she* needs from a relationship. She utilizes the relationship exercises I have given her and then, together, we concretely identify what behaviors she is looking for from a significant other. This gives her the opportunity to assert her need for these behaviors. Instead of feeling guilt, she is now learning to set boundaries. And instead of being angry with her boyfriend when he goes out drinking and uses her debit card when they are struggling financially and he is not working, she no longer permits him to use her card and holds him responsible to carry his own weight in the relationship. Significant progress, happiness, and emotional stability were increasingly apparent.

Treatment

After obtaining a history and a review of the client's reason for referral—i.e., why they are here and what they want to change—we begin the *process* of change. We discuss their strengths and weaknesses, develop a genogram, which is similar to a family tree, identify communication patterns learned from their past, and then set goals that will get them out of the delusion they have created. The treatment plan is then written up and, as a team, we develop new skills that get us to the completion of treatment and free from the discomfort.

In this situation, using CBT logs and NFB assisted the client with thought shifting. Please refer to the treatment plan to review the treatment goals and objectives.

Dependency

Client Name: _____ Date: _____

Problem 1: Dependency

Long Term Goal:
To begin the development of an independent self that is able to meet some of her/his needs and tolerate being alone

Short Term Goals (STG):
1. Identify and clarify own emotional and social needs.   **Target Date:** _____
2. Develop a clear-cut set of limits for self and not take responsibility for other's behavior and feelings.   **Target Date:** _____
3. Identify and set new boundaries for self in key life relationships   **Target Date:** _____
4. _____

Procedures/Methods:
   STG 1: Ask client to put together a list of their needs and ways that these could possibly be met. Process list with therapist.
   STG 2: Assist client in developing new ways to set and implement boundaries and limits for self
   STG 3: Ask client to read literature or view educational films that focus on dependency, such as boundaries and relationships and process with therapist.
   STG 4: _____

Measurable Indicators:
   STG 1: Written and verbal reports and process with therapist
   STG 2: Self-report and process with therapist
   STG 3: Didactic discussion of book with therapist
   STG 4: _____

Client Signature: _____

Counselor Signature: _____

Chapter 7

The Shame Delusion

Shame is in many ways the sibling of guilt. The difference between the two emotional states is sometimes difficult to see, but an easy way to distinguish them is by thinking about guilt as an emotion that arises when we have done something by act or omission that goes against our internal code of right behavior. Shame, on the other hand, is the emotion we feel when we perceive (rightly or wrongly) that we have transgressed some societal or cultural value—an externally imposed standard of "right" or "proper" behavior.

Over the last 30 years, there has been a new focus on shame by the psychotherapeutic establishment as it has become more and more evident that shame plays a central role in many of today's addictions. Shame can be found at the heart of maladaptive behaviors such as alcoholism, drug abuse, eating disorders, and many abusive behaviors, to name but a few shame-related disorders. (Gershen Kaufman, *The Psychology of Shame: Theory and Treatment of Shame Based Syndromes.* New York: Springer Publishing Co., 1996.) Indeed, shame has been characterized as a "master emotion," regulating the expression of many other feelings. Unlike other emotions whose impact normally diminishes over time, shame is the most difficult emotion for an individual to admit and let go of. It is also the most private of emotions.

Shame is found in every culture in every part of the world. On its positive side, it is an important societal tool used to further the goals of the society and to exert control over its members. Shame is extraordinarily important in that it helps to shape the individual's conscience. It alerts us to our misconduct or wrongdoing and motivates us to self-correct our bad behavior. In this regard, it can be considered in a positive light as a fundamentally "civilizing" force. However, overdevelopment or underdevelopment of the shame component in our personality may lead to behavior disorders.

Some individuals who were raised in overly strict environments and who absorbed shame-based messages from caregivers or other central figures in their early years have a high likelihood of developing issues with self-esteem, body image, self-doubt, insecurities, or low self-confidence. These in turn will create deep feelings of inferiority. When an individual feels shame, the entire self is involved—as opposed to issues of guilt, in which only the act or misdeed is the focus of the individual's attention. This is the reason shame can be the far more harmful of the two emotional states. A person can feel badly about committing some bad act or deed, but the negative self-feeling is generally limited to that discrete incident. Guilt does not lead to the intense feelings of self-loathing that shame brings with it. Shame is an all-pervasive negative feeling about one's entire personhood, one's being. It is therefore far more profound, and, as a consequence, has the potential to be a much more damaging negative emotional state than guilt.

Negative behaviors

Looking at shame at work within a family system, it is easy to see how shame can wound not only the individual carrying it but also his or her interpersonal relationships. The parent-child relationship, marital relationship, and others may end up in a highly dysfunctional state leading to negative behaviors such as child abuse or spousal abuse. This is particularly true when shaming is used as a weapon. Violence generally escalates dramatically in this atmosphere, leading to all sorts of domestic crimes with the attendant consequences.

Addiction can almost always be viewed as shame-based. Shame and addiction are deeply intertwined. Alcoholics and others suffering from addictive behavior are prone to shame, perhaps by disposition. The addictive behaviors help the individual numb these painful feelings. Drinking, drugging, engaging in eating disorders and similar negative behavior measures are all used to cope with feelings of chronic shame and low self-worth. Similarly, the drinking and drugging cause more shame and self-loathing, creating a vicious cycle of self-abuse. Shame is more and more becoming recognized as a central emotional state responsible for most, if not all, addictive behaviors.

Case history

The day that J.T. walked through my office door, I couldn't help but be struck by the 27-year-old's quintessentially all-American good looks, charm, and articulateness. The product of exclusive Manhattan private schooling, he had spent every summer—virtually from birth—at his grandparents' Maine home. A tremendously gifted young actor, he had been accepted by the highly prestigious Julliard School, which he attended for two and a half years. Hence, on paper, no one could have had more going for him on the path to enormous success. However, anyone familiar with the disease of addiction and its many manifestations will not be surprised to learn the dark turn he took on the road of life as a result.

Born into a family where alcoholism didn't just run through it but rather galloped, J.T. had sadly fallen prey to the bleak forces of this insidious disease at a very early age. At 15, he overdosed on a combination of his grandmother's painkillers and his grandfather's scotch. And it was all downhill from that point on. Six rehabs, multiple detoxes, scores of broken promises and lost dreams later, he and his family had all but given up any glimmer of hope that he would ever come close to fulfilling the "golden boy" potential that had seemed his destiny virtually from day one. As a last-ditch effort, he was referred to me.

Diagnosed as learning disabled with dyslexia and attention deficit disorder at the age of seven, J.T. had been prescribed medication to address these conditions from early on (although his mother stopped the Ritalin after only two months when she observed adverse effects in him). His inability to focus made him prone to self-medicate by whatever means he could find. At school he was made a laughingstock by his fellow classmates, which only served to further shame this otherwise gifted young man.

Given the privileged backgrounds of the friends who surrounded him, he had easy access to all manner of street drugs and alcohol. In spite of his considerable talent and success with acting, his constant struggles in the academic realm and persistent behavioral problems throughout his formative years had left him with an extremely low sense of self-esteem and a great deal of shame.

Antidepressants had been part of his life from an early age, as had various forms of psychotherapy. None of this had any lasting effect on J.T. In our first visit, it was apparent that he was on the verge of suicide, so my first order of business was to have him evaluated by one of my psychiatrist colleagues who specialize in adolescent cases. A complete review of J.T.'s medication regime was done and my MD colleague confirmed what I had initially suspected—he was on the wrong medications. J.T.'s medications were corrected and it then became possible for me to begin treating him.

Having had a great deal of success in recent years with neurofeedback, I administered 20 sessions to J.T. with remarkable results. And although the concept of "homework" made him recoil in horror because of his less than pleasant experiences with school, I made sure he didn't leave our appointments without promising to complete the "assignment" I gave him. He was to bring his completed assignment with him to our next session.

Our initial session, in addition to taking his medication history, focused on taking a complete psychosocial assessment as well as basic family history. The following sessions included J.T. setting goals for himself, based on *acting* and not *re*acting to life, which had always been his MO. The main points I asked him to think carefully about for our next session included:

- Living life on *its* terms and not his own.
- Recognizing the fact that we are all born alone and no one is responsible for your life but *you*.
- The easier life is, ironically, the less quality of it you will have.
- What does this all mean? It means that if you do not work for what you want, you will not have the satisfaction you are seeking. A good example of this is the story of the Three Little Pigs. The House of Straw and Sticks is built more quickly and

easily and gets blown away when adversity hits. However, the House of Bricks withstands the test of potential destruction and remains intact in the end.

His first assignment was to begin a journal in which he was to answer the following questions:

1. What goals do you have that you believe are realistically attainable?
2. What do you honestly expect out of your life?

Treatment

After obtaining a history and a review of the client's reason for referral—i.e., why they are here and what they want to change—we begin the *process* of change. We discuss their strengths and weaknesses, develop a genogram, which is similar to a family tree, identify communication patterns learned from their past, and then set goals that will get them out of the delusion they have created. The treatment plan is then written up and, as a team, we develop new skills that get us to the completion of treatment and free from the discomfort.

The use of CBT logs and NFB was helpful to assist with cognitive reframing. The accompanying treatment plan shows the goals and objectives established.

Then we begin the process of logging how and why we *react* rather than *respond* to our situations and what delusions we choose to deal with, and how instead to challenge these delusions in order to see the truth.

Dual Diagnosis tx plan

Client Name: _____   Date:_____

Problem 1: Dual Diagnosis Issues
Specify mental health & substance abuse issues here –
_____

Long Term Goal: To manage simultaneously substance abuse and mental health issues so that healthy functioning in the realms of home, work and relationships are achieved.

Short Term Goals (STG):
   1. To learn about how alcohol/drug dependence can perpetuate and worsen existing depression, anxiety, suicidality, and other mental health issues   **Target Date: _____**
   2. To identify and practice positive, healthier new coping skills for dealing with depressive thoughts and personal stress/anxiety in lieu of drinking/using   **Target Date: _____**
   3. Develop and practice social skills without the aid of substances   **Target Date: _____**
   4. Work towards abstinence and an effective relapse prevention plan **Target Date: _____**
   5. _____

Procedures/Methods:
STG 1: Ask the client to read literature or view educational films about dual diagnosis and the interplay between depression/anxiety and alcohol/drug dependence and discuss several key concepts in therapy.
STG 2: The client will be assisted in identifying high risk situations that cause strong cravings and self-harm impulses and will be asked to list and discuss distractions, relaxation, and positive self-talk affirmation to detour out of the cycle.
STG 3: Client will be encouraged to attend AA/NA and other recovery groups and also to develop a support network of non-users and non-alcoholics
STG 4: List and discuss in therapy sessions the negative effects of drinking/using and also list and discuss the key life changes that are necessary for clean and sober living
STG 5: _____

Measurable Indicators:
STG 1: Self-report of increased knowledge about dual diagnosis
STG 2: Process in therapy and self-report of increased ability to use alternative coping skills in crisis situations
STG 3: Self-report and therapist's observation
STG 4: Process in therapy
STG 5: _____

Client Signature: _____

Counselor Signature: _____

56

Chapter 8

Addictions

Addiction is often referred to as a physical or mental condition occurring when an individual ingests a substance like alcohol, cannabis, or cocaine, or compulsively pursues an activity like indiscriminate sex or gambling to such an extent that it becomes habitual and begins to seriously interfere with the his daily affairs and responsibilities. Such individuals may become so habituated to their addictive behaviors that they are unaware that these behaviors are leading to real problems in their lives.

Addiction is a complex area. In part this is due to the fact that it generally contains both a physical and a psychological component. On the physical side, there is the chemical interaction of the body with the substance that produces the euphoric effect. Over time, the body develops a tolerance so that more of the substance is required to achieve the same level of "high." This tolerance creates a withdrawal condition when the substance is not ingested for a period of time. Withdrawal is usually painful and can be dangerous if not medically supervised. There is also a psychological side to addiction that relates to the individual's formation of associations with various parts of his or her life that involved using the substance or being under its influence. The brain forms these associations over time, and these psychological attachments become another major hurdle for the addict to overcome on the road to recovery.

Most addictive behaviors start out as coping mechanisms to numb the individual's anxiety or emotional stress. This is true for substance addiction as well as other addictive behavior like gambling and obsessive sexual activities. These are primarily psychologically based addictions since they do not require using substances. There may be similarities in the euphoric effects they produce, but there is not a chemical interaction with the body. Though it is certainly true that some addictions will destroy the addict quicker than others and are therefore looked at as more harmful, the truth of the matter is that all addictions pose serious health, interpersonal, employment, and legal issues that may end up killing the addict if left untreated. Treating any addiction requires an understanding of the psychological dynamics involved as well as any medical implications.

The addict is generally looked down on by society, and many see addiction as caused by a lack of character or some moral defect. However, experts have learned that the root causes of addiction have nothing to do with a person's "character." Though there may be a genetic predisposition to addiction in one's family, the primary cause is the person's inability to manage stress and anxiety in a normal way. For whatever reasons, he or she discovered a substance or behavior that alleviated their negative emotional state, even if only for a short time.

The debate will continue between the medical and psychological communities as to whether addiction is a disease or a mental illness, or whether it is caused by a genetic defect, for example, as well as any number of other issues. In fact, these debates will continue for many years because there is no clear-cut answer to these questions, and most of the time there is a mix of both physical and psychological causes for addiction. No matter what the origin of an individual's addiction, the good news today is that the medical and psychotherapeutic communities have many treatment tools to use, and treatment programs are getting better all the time. In the optimum situation, a person's treatment will include a medically supervised component to deal with safe withdrawal and the ongoing administration of medications to enforce substance avoidance, and a psychotherapeutic component to help the individual learn the underlying reasons for his or her behavior and provide stress- and anxiety-reduction tools.

Negative behaviors

Most all of the negative human behaviors one can think of can be caused by addiction-related behaviors. Innumerable traffic accidents, thefts, acts of violence, and other antisocial conduct can be traced to addictive be-havior. The National Institute on Drug Abuse has estimated that the total annual cost of alcohol and drug abuse in America is about $524 billion. This is a huge number and reflects the tragic consequences and costs to society of the associated health care, productivity loss, crime, incarcera-tion, and law-enforcement activities addiction leads to in our society. The other hidden costs of addiction are the countless broken homes, child and spousal abuse, job loss, bankruptcy, and premature death. The human and societal toll taken by addictions every year is heartbreaking and breathtaking in its scope.

Case history

José is what I consider to be one of the lucky ones when it comes to ultimately facing his addiction and the other delusions it brings with it. Sadly, the seeds of the control delusion through the use of substances are sewn very early on. When a young child senses from the start that the world around him is simply out of control, he seeks infantile ways in which to cope—most frequently by trying to control the parts of his life he feels he *can* control. Usually this involves the child becoming overly obsessed with areas he or she believes are within his power to rule. Never fully maturing emotionally, he remains stuck in this childlike manner of coping, which inevitably leads to a lifelong pattern that, while it may have served as a sort of "balm" in childhood, only serves in adulthood to further distance him from the lives that mean the most to him.

Abandoned by his father at the age of eight, José was raised by his mother and a maternal aunt; hence he assumed a survivalist mentality, convinced that he was on his own in this world and *must get through it* solely and totally by himself. As such, he purposely developed no attach-ments to other people or places (perceiving that they would weigh him down), living only in the moment, all the while looking for situations and others he believed could "quick-fix" his needs. As a result, the coping mechanisms for his ever-increasing aggression and the rearing of ADHD became, predictably, the use—and quickly the abuse—of substances.

It was only recently, when he became aware that he had become a father that the light for change began to flicker and increasingly burn as a possibility for escape from a world that had only known darkness. The relationship with his son became his motivation for reevaluating his lifestyle and desperately seeking a way in which he could rectify his early childhood maladaptations. Hence, he sought my counsel and was ready and willing (as only a "drowning man" can truly be) to let the healing begin. Through our sessions together, this 25-year-old Hispanic man/child began to grow by challenging his beliefs with regard to his mistrust of others. A crucially important first step. From there, our work together enabled him to change his outlook from merely surviving life to actually *living* it, thereby allowing him to teach his son, through his example, the life skills necessary to have a better quality of interpersonal relationships and vastly improved self-confidence than José ever knew could exist, much less experience himself.

Along our journey together, José utilized the work of Ruiz's Four Agreements, and was guided through our sessions to understand ways in which he could challenge his automatic reactions to conflict (i.e., aggressive behaviors/manipulation). He went on to learn ways in which to shift his thought process so that he could be positively and productively responsive to situations, without having them trigger the familiar emotions related to being a "have-not."

In the end, José began making better choices in relationships and, thankfully, found the strength through a belief in a Higher Power, supported by therapy and a twelve-step program to stop using drugs. These tools also afforded him the opportunity to make better, saner, and more grounded decisions when it came to relationships, and he was finally able to relinquish his seat on the quick-fix train. As a natural consequence and tremendous benefit of this enormous shift in behavior and outlook, he was much better equipped to control his aggressive knee-jerk reactions to the problems we all encounter on this journey known as life. As a glorious result, he didn't have to repeat the only modeling of fatherhood he had ever experienced and, very thankfully, was able to connect on an emotional level with his son, giving him a fighting chance to live the kind of life God intended for him.

Today, the father-son interaction is like poetry in motion, and I'm proud to have played a small part in facilitating that. Patients like José are the reason I do (and will continue doing) what I do, for there is no price that can be put on the satisfaction I derive for having played a part in breaking the family cycle of severe dysfunction, ensuring that a son and future generations will have a fighting chance at happiness (with a respective nod to free will).

Treatment

After obtaining a history and a review of the client's reason for referral—i.e., why they are here and what they want to change—we begin the *process* of change. We discuss their strengths and weaknesses, develop a genogram, which is similar to a family tree, identify communication patterns learned from their past, and then set goals that will get them out of the delusion they have created. The treatment plan is then written up and, as a team, we develop new skills that get us to the completion of treatment and free from the discomfort.

These treatment plans addressed identifying the role drug use played in fueling José's delusions. CBT and NFB where modalities used, and in the treatment plan you can examine the goals and objectives addressed in the treatment process.

Dual Diagnosis tx plan

Client Name: _____   Date:_____

Problem 1: Dual Diagnosis Issues
Specify mental health & substance abuse issues here –
_____

Long Term Goal: To manage simultaneously substance abuse and mental health issues so that healthy functioning in the realms of home, work and relationships are achieved.

Short Term Goals (STG):
   1. To learn about how alcohol/drug dependence can perpetuate and worsen existing depression, anxiety, suicidality, and other mental health issues   **Target Date:** _____
   2. To identify and practice positive, healthier new coping skills for dealing with depressive thoughts and personal stress/anxiety in lieu of drinking/using   **Target Date:** _____
   3. Develop and practice social skills without the aid of substances   **Target Date:** _____
   4. Work towards abstinence and an effective relapse prevention plan **Target Date:** _____
   5. _____

Procedures/Methods:
   STG 1: Ask the client to read literature or view educational films about dual diagnosis and the interplay between depression/anxiety and alcohol/drug dependence and discuss several key concepts in therapy.
   STG 2: The client will be assisted in identifying high risk situations that cause strong cravings and self-harm impulses and will be asked to list and discuss distractions, relaxation, and positive self-talk affirmation to detour out of the cycle.
   STG 3: Client will be encouraged to attend AA/NA and other recovery groups and also to develop a support network of non-users and non-alcoholics
   STG 4: List and discuss in therapy sessions the negative effects of drinking/using and also list and discuss the key life changes that are necessary for clean and sober living
   STG 5: _____

Measurable Indicators:
STG 1: Self-report of increased knowledge about dual diagnosis
STG 2: Process in therapy and self-report of increased ability to use alternative coping skills in crisis situations
STG 3: Self-report and therapist's observation
STG 4: Process in therapy
STG 5: _____

Client Signature: _____

Counselor Signature: _____

Adjustment Disorder tx plan

Client Name _____ Date: _____

Problem 1: Adjustment Disorder issues pertaining to the following identifiable stressor and causing the following emotional, behavioral, and social symptoms –

_____

Long Term Goal: To alleviate the distress triggered by the above event and improve general coping

Short Term Goals (STG)

1. To vent thoughts and feelings associated with the change or loss and receive supportive feedback **Target Date:_____**
2. To identify and counter negative self-talk that exacerbates the maladaptive reaction to the above stressor **Target Date: _____**
3. To develop healthy coping strategies and identify alternative ways of managing and resolving issues **Target Date:_____**
4. Boost self-confidence and optimism by identifying personals assets/strengths and external resources for healing **Target Date:_____**
5. _____**Target Date: _____**

Procedure/Methods:

    STG 1: Exploration of thoughts and feelings in sessions and journal writing or "homework assignments" in between sessions

    STG 2: Therapist will introduce the concept of "self-talk" and help to identify maladaptive thinking patterns and positive counter statements/affirmations

    STG 3: Therapist will assist the client in identifying (verbally and on paper) ideas for self-care and positive management of symptoms and help them rearrange their daily schedules to allow for the practice of these positive coping strategies

    STG 4: The client will identify (verbally and on paper) inner and external resources for healing and will review in sessions methods for successful coping in past life transitions

    STG 5: _____

Measurable Indicators:

    STG 1: The client regularly attends therapy sessions, verbalizes the impact of the event on their life and mood, and is receptive to supportive feedback

    STG 2: Process in therapy and self-report of increased awareness of the impact of thinking patterns on their behavior and mood.

    STG 3: The client self-reports the ability to use alternative coping skills in real life situations

    STG 4: Process in therapy and self-report of being able to draw on existing strengths to adjust to the change and loss

Client Signature:_____ Counselor Signature: _____

Chapter 9

My Treatment Methods

All delusions are challenged by utilizing Cognitive Behavioral Therapy. This technique has the person ask the question, "Are my thoughts/feelings/behaviors rooted in facts or fiction?" This treatment approach is a check-up from the head up.

The patient tries to figure out why he or she is unhappy. It is time for the patient to overcome his unproductive patterns of thinking. These have been acquired by habit or inherited. When the patient learns to shift them, he will be content and live in truth. He will be proactive versus self-destructive and be more responsive versus reactive.

Once the main symptoms are identified, such as anxiety, depression, codependency, addiction, etc., goals and objectives are set. When this is done, the work begins.

Keeping a journal or log is the first assignment:

Step one: The patient writes down a situation that triggers an uncomfortable feeling, and then we rate that feeling. **Step two:** We identify the automatic negative thought(s) that the feeling triggers, which is the foundation of the delusion the patient is living in. (What is going through your mind when the uncomfortable feeling happens?) Examples of negative thoughts can be that judging oneself or another as good or bad, right or wrong, etc. Or maybe blaming that focuses on others as the source of the negative feeling. Or perhaps using "should" and not focusing on what *could* be. **Step three:** Ask the question, "Is it based in fact or fiction?" (What is a fact based in? Concrete evidence. Fiction is assuming and making a belief a fact. For example, a person not talking to you is a fact; assuming they are not talking to you because they don't like you is a belief and may be a fiction. **Step four:** Ask "Is there evidence to support this belief, or is it my assumption or emotional reaction?" **Step five:** Try to shift the negative thought fed by the inaccurate belief. Substitute more realistic thoughts. For example, most things others do are not about you, but about them and where they are emotionally. **Step six:** Rate the feeling and see if it decreased in intensity.

Continue this process until we've established the ability to thought-shift away from the delusions and see the truth, and be able to utilize positive self-talk to reinforce the truth and become more responsive.

CBT differs from traditional talking therapy in several respects:
- **Length.** Unlike psychoanalysis, which can last for years, the average number of CBT sessions is 16. The length of the therapy is often determined in advance, at the beginning of treatment.
- **Structure.** Most CBT therapists have a "lesson plan" for each session that includes a set of specific techniques and goals for the patient to learn.
- **Homework.** More so than other forms of therapy, CBT requires the patient to actively identify the triggers of their negative thinking and to "practice" alternative responses. Patients may be asked to keep a journal of their thoughts or to actively schedule challenging situations for themselves.

CBT is and has been my modality of treatment. In 2009 I added neurofeedback to the treatment process. It works directly in assisting the brain to self-regulate. *Neurofeedback* is direct training of brain function for self-regulation, a necessary part of good brain function. Neurofeedback heals the brain. Psychotherapy heals the mind. Together, neurotherapy and psychotherapy can create lasting change and recovery. As the brain heals, the patient can better engage in the psychotherapy process and make more conscious, healthy decisions for himself.

Neurofeedback trains the brain to optimize its brainwave patterns, which results in self-healing. Results include increased attention and focus, emotional stability, inner calm, a quiet mind, and the resiliency to cope with the stresses of daily life.

This brain's activity occurs in four distinctive brainwave patterns, from very slow to very fast. Recent research shows that individuals with conditions such as ADHD, anxiety, sleep difficulties, and other conditions have brainwave activity that is either too slow or too fast. For example, people with ADHD have less activity in areas of the brain that control focus, attention, and the regulation of behavior and emotion.

Research also shows that when we train our brain with neurofeedback, it will correct faulty brainwave activity. It "exercises" the areas of the brain that control attention, emotion, focus, and behavior, and therefore strengthens these areas, resulting in reduction or elimination of symptoms.

The following are adjunct therapies that I suggest to my patients. These adjunct therapies are ways that my patients take personal responsibility for maintaining the thought shifts, behavior changes, and emotional shifts that have helped them come out of their delusion and live in truth.

Mindfulness meditation is currently all the rage and it works. But it cannot treat (or cure) mental illness by itself.

Meditation is a powerful tool when used to decrease stress and increase well-being. But if we are to maintain that mental illnesses are biochemical malfunctions of the brain and nervous system, then we must allow room in treatment for medicine. Therapy also has a long history of positive impact on the lives of those challenged by psychiatric disease. Meditation, when added to more traditional and well-tested methods of treatment, can help a patient successfully manage a challenging life.

There is emerging evidence from randomized trials to support popular beliefs about yoga for depression, sleep disorders, and as an augmentation therapy. Limitations of the literature include inability to do double-blind studies, a multiplicity of comparisons within small studies, and lack of replication. Biomarker and neuroimaging studies, those comparing yoga with standard pharmaco- and psychotherapies, and studies of long-term efficacy are needed to fully translate the promise of yoga for enhancing mental health.

There is a connection between *qigong* and mental health. This connection is both obvious and subtle. On the most surface level, learning to relax and to move in a relaxed manner has many mental health payoffs:

- Tension and stress can be coped with more effectively when one is relaxed
- Moving with more balance and body awareness increases self-confidence.
- Some people find tai chi and qigong to enhance their spiritual life and practice; spirituality often is associated with improved mental health.
- The styles of qigong and tai chi (Sun style) are easily adaptable for anyone's skill level or physical limitations—the styles can be modified and learned by world-class athletes or persons limited to wheelchair practice. Thus, the "I can't do this" factor is eliminated. Persons with little or no athletic prowess can engage in a movement activity that has the grace of dance, the relaxation of meditation, and the movement of martial arts. Again, this enhances self-esteem and self-confidence.

An additional set of mental health benefits can result from the practice of deep abdominal (qigong) breathing:

- The relaxation and sense of well-being attained by deep breathing are well-documented to have positive effects on overall health and a sense of well-being.
- The "breathwork," in conjunction with guided imagery, focused prayer, or other healing approaches can positively affect the outcomes of treatment of anxiety and anxiety disorders, such as PTSD, generalized anxiety, and phobias.
- Deep breathing is also helpful in treating depression.

Music has a special ability to pump us up or calm us down. Scientists are still trying to figure out what's going on in our brains when we listen to music and how it produces such potent effects on the psyche.

"We're using music to better understand brain function in general," says Daniel Levitin, a prominent psychologist who studies the neuroscience of music at McGill University in Montreal. Listening to music feels good, but can that translate into physiological benefit? Levitin and colleagues have published 400 studies in the journal *Trends in Cognitive Sciences*, suggesting that the answer is yes.

In one study reviewed, researchers studied patients who were about to undergo surgery. Participants were randomly assigned to either listen to music or take antianxiety drugs. Scientists tracked patients' ratings of their own anxiety, as well as the levels of the stress hormone cortisol. The results: The patients who listened to music had less anxiety and lower cortisol than people who took drugs. Levitin cautions that this is only one study, and more research needs to be done to confirm the results, but it points toward a powerful medicinal use for music.

"The promise here is that music is arguably less expensive than drugs, and it's easier on the body and doesn't have side effects," Levitin says.

Another technique is called *biofeedback*, and the therapy is used to help prevent or treat conditions including migraine headaches, chronic pain, incontinence, and high blood pressure.

During a biofeedback session, electrodes are attached to your skin. These electrodes send signals to a monitor, which displays a sound, flash of light, or image that represents your heart and breathing rate, blood pressure, skin temperature, sweating, or muscle activity.

When you're under stress, these functions change. Your heart rate speeds up, your muscles tighten, your blood pressure rises, you start to sweat, and your breathing quickens. You can see these stress responses as they happen on the monitor, and then get immediate feedback as you try to stop them.

A biofeedback therapist helps you practice relaxation exercises, which you fine-tune to control different body functions. For example, you might use a relaxation technique to turn down the brainwaves that activate when you have a headache.

Several different relaxation exercises are used in biofeedback therapy, including:

- Deep breathing
- Progressive muscle relaxation—alternately tightening and then relaxing different muscle groups

- Guided imagery—concentrating on a specific image (such as the color and texture of an orange) to focus your mind and make you feel more relaxed
- Mindfulness meditation—focusing your thoughts and letting go of negative emotions

Using Eric Erikson's stages of development theory helps me assess and identify where a client may be in his emotional development. This can be a valuable tool for establishing a treatment plan (see chart that follows).

From Wikipedia (accessed 8/23/14): A *genogram* (also known as a McGoldrick-Gerson Study) is a pictorial display of a person's family relationships and medical history. It goes beyond a traditional family tree by allowing the user to visualize hereditary patterns and psychological factors that impact relationships. It can be used to identify repetitive patterns of behavior and to recognize hereditary tendencies.

In the Appendix section there are samples of exercises and techniques involving the various adjunct therapies mentioned above. As noted in the previous chapters, I have recommended these techniques to all my clients at some point in the treatment process to assist them with achieving their treatment goals.

Genogram

IV. Family Chart/Genogram

GRAND-PARENTS   Paternal   Maternal

_____   _____

PGF	PGM	MGF	MGM
Name_____	Name _____	Name _____	Name _____
Birth	Birth	Birth	Birth
Death	Death	Death	Death

PARENTS   Father --- Mother

                          Name _____   Name _____

                          Birth   Birth

SELF/SIBLINGS   --

Client's Name_____

Date of Birth_____

In the above chart please fill as much information as you have for the names, dates of birth and death, school and marital status.

Write in, where relevant, the occurrences of significant historical data such as:

medical/physical symptoms	illegitimacies
emotional /psychiatric symptoms	drugs or alcohol abuse
premature deaths	social difficulties/school /drop-out/peers
suicides	problem leaving home or parents
separations or divorces	financial/employment difficulties
legal/police involvement	

Please add a written summary about family background that you feel would be helpful for developing a treatment plan for your child. Feel free to use the back of this form if additional space is needed.

Name of person filling out the form_____

Date _____

Chapter 10

Conclusion

As I reflect on my story and the stories of others, I see that if we really take a look, if we stop and identify what we are feeling, we can become aware of what has been triggered by some event in our lives. We can then listen closely to what we automatically start saying to ourselves. By doing this, we flush out the delusion. Then and only then can we challenge these delusions and separate fact from the fiction we've created. We tend to make excuses and ignore the truth when swept away with our delusions. Once we come out of the delusion we can prepare for the foundation of truth one step at a time.

The more aware we become of our basic maps (assumptions) and the extent to which we have been influenced by them, the more we can take responsibility for those paradigms that have been created out of reactions. We break out of boxes that block our growth and then see the distortions/lies/delusions. Finally, then, we can examine them against reality. By stopping and really looking, we get a more objective/panoramic view. That is what clarity "really is" and what "being focused" really means. No quick fixes, no quick looks. If any response is quick then we have missed something. It isn't a response, it is a reaction—and now we know the difference. Responses are connected/based on reality. Reactions are flights into fantasy.

We are creatures of habit, habit being a *learned* reaction to external stimuli compared to instinct, which is a *natural* reaction to external stimuli. As we increase our learned reactions through time and experience, we move further away from our natural reactions. Some of the layers of learned reactions over the natural reactions are necessary for survival within the rules of a complex societal structure.

I feel there are two distinct types of non-natural or learned habits, the first being what I call casual habits. Casual habits are ones that we are aware of and have had an active part in generating. Casual habits can be changed through gradual behavior modification. Smoking, watching sitcoms, the times we start our day, are all examples of casual habits.

The second type of learned habits I call foundation habits or delusions. These habits are started at a very young age and become part of the very foundation of who we are and will become in the future. As we develop who we are in life, we build the stories of our "house." If we have a round foundation, we will build a round house. The further down the road of life we travel, the more stories. As we increase the stories, the further away from the foundation we become until we reach the point of no longer being aware of the nature of our foundation or why we have a round house. We just consider it as a natural part of ourselves. It becomes who we are in reality. It is!

But what if we need to change one of those foundation habits because it has become a detriment to what we choose to be, or it conflicts with a natural or instinctive habit? If we attempt to alter it by altering one or more of the floors of our house, the alteration will gradually follow the original foundation and design. It would be like taking floors of a round house and trying to make it square. To make it fit with the rest of the house, we would gradually and eventually "rebuild" the floor round.

The reality is that to change the nature and design of the house, we must tear down everything built above the foundation, rebuild the foundation, then rebuild the house based on the new foundation's design. For most people, this is almost impossible to do, for it means living for a while without a house—without a past and without a clear future. It means removing the familiar and secure. It means actively and totally destroying who we are. This cannot be done gradually over time like changing a casual habit or we will just rebuild to the design of the foundation that we are trying to change. The house must be traumatically destroyed in one decisive blow to get immediately to the foundation. This is what is needed to come out of our delusional thoughts—the thoughts that trigger reactive habits that create our disillusionment and discomfort.

The methods I have been discussing help us come out of the dark. They help us identify the difference between a reaction and a response. By changing your paradigm, you make the conscious decision to live in truth and will begin to find contentment and inner peace. Finally, the types of methods I use with my clients are determined by their presenting issues, which are the symptoms of their delusion. Their level of motivation and comfort level with the treatment options offered, and their ability to feel respected and in turn trust the process, are what will make all the difference between success and failure.

The future of psychotherapy is very exciting. Clients no longer want to "just" talk. They are looking for an interactive experience. The merging of cognitive behavioral therapy and EEG neurofeedback does just that. I agree with the belief of Siegfried Othmer, who wrote, back in 2002:

> In the future, EEG neurofeedback will not be seen so much as a treatment for ADHD, seizures, depression, and addictions as it will be seen as a generic tool for the improvement of the brain's capacity for self-regulation. In consequence of which many symptoms filling the DSM-IV will yield their conceptual hold on us, the DSM-IV construct will be eclipsed. The diagnostic preoccupation of the current generation of practitioners will fade with emergence of comprehensive models of brain function—and of dysfunction—of elegant simplicity. Such models will lay the basis for the observation that a very simple set of neurofeedback tools can address a wide variety of disorders.

*   *   *   *

So how do you find the right therapist who can provide you with the right tools and whom you can trust? Do your homework. The key to finding the right therapist is to first find someone who has expertise in the type of treatment you are seeking. Word of mouth is the best way. Ask your friends and family who they know. If all else fails, "Google it." Call around and seek a consultation with a therapist to see if your personalities fit. Finally, look for a therapist who can and will give you an outline or roadmap called a treatment plan that gives you an overview of what the goals and objectives will be and is willing to adjust it based on your needs and input. You don't build a house without a floor plan, right? You are the designer/client and the therapist is your contractor. He or she works for you and with you. Most importantly, remember that personal growth is a Journey to your Heart.

REFERENCES

The Birth Order Book by Dr. Kevin Leman

Born to Rebel by Frank J. Sullaway

Family Therapy in Clinical Practice by Murray Bowen

Family Development by Evelyn Duvall

Family Therapy and Sibling Position by Walter Toman

"Psychodynamics of Normal and Neurotic Perfectionism" by D. E. Hamachek, in *Psychology: A Journal of Human Behavior*

The Psychology of Shame by Gershen Kaufman

A Symphony in the Brain by Jim Robbins

"EEG Biofeedback as a Modality for Treating Addiction"

by Siegfried Othmer, Ph.D., & Mark Steinberg, Ph.D., on eeginfo.com

The Neuroscience of Psychotherapy by Louis Cozolino

Heal Yourself with Qigong by Suzanne Friedman, LaC, DMQ

"Ready, Aim…Oh Well" by Martha Beck, in *O Magazine*, July 2003

Wherever You Go, There You Are by Jon Kabat-Zinn

The Power of Now by Eckhart Tolle

You Can Heal Your Life by Louise Hay

The Four Agreements by Don Miquel Ruiz

The Tao of Music by John M. Ortiz

Making a Good Brain Great by Daniel Amen, MD

The REBT Resource Book for Practitioners, Bernard & Wolfe, eds.:

written by Albert Ellis

The Feeling Good Handbook by David D. Burns, MD

Shame and Guilt: Masters of Disguise by Jane Middleton-Moz

The Self-Esteem Guided Journal by Matthew McKay, Ph.D.

A Gift to Myself by Charles L. Whitfield

The Three Minute Meditator by David Harp & Nina Smiley

Meditation for Life by Martine Batcheior

Mindfulness Yoga: The Awakened Union of Breath, Body, and Mind by Georg Feuerstein

The Woman's Retreat Book by Jennifer Louden

Cognitive Behavioral Therapy: Treatment of Difficult and Complex Cases

by Drs. Arthur and Sharon Morgillo Freedman

eeginfo.com

helptheself.com

Fact or Fiction... How to Eliminate Negative Thoughts

Check up from the Head Up

Well here we are once again. We are trying to figure out, "Why does my life suck" or, "Why can't I be happy"? So hear this. It is time to identify, challenge and overcome your unproductive patterns of thinking. You have acquired them by habit or inherited them. When you learn to shift them is when you will be happy. Let's learn ways to become more proactive vs self-destructive. Let's be more responsive vs reactive to our life. Let's start now.

Keep a Daily Thoughts Journal using the following steps.

STEP ONE: Write down a situation that triggers your unhappy or uncomfortable feeling (such as an incident that makes you feel abandoned or scared or angry). Rate how strong the feeling is from 1 to 5 (1 – not strong to 5 - overwhelming).

STEP TWO: Then evaluate the automatic negative thoughts that the feeling triggers (What was going through your mind when the feeling happened). Examples of negative thoughts can be that you judge yourself or others as black and white – i.e. good or bad, right or wrong, "what if" and "yeah but" responses to the situation thereby blocking a solution. Or maybe it is blaming – focusing on others as the source of your negative feeling, or using "should" and not focusing on "what is". Only looking at the negatives and discounting the positives of a situation is another example. These are just a few small samples of distortions but a good start.

STEP THREE: Ask the question about the thought as follows – Fact or Fiction? Fact is based on concrete evidence. Fiction is assuming – i.e. making your own belief. Example: Fact – A person is not talking to you. May be fiction – Assuming that it is because he or she doesn't like you.

STEP FOUR: Ask yourself if there is evidence to support this belief or is it based on your assumptions or emotional reactions?

STEP FIVE: Try to shift the negative thought fed by the inaccurate belief. Substitute it with more realistic thoughts such as: "most of the things others do are not about me. It's about them and where they are emotionally".

STEP SIX: Re-rate your feeling and see if it has increased or decreased in intensity.

Try this and send me your results, feedback or questions.

Thoughts and Feelings Worksheet

The Situation: _____

_____

_____

_____

_____

_____

Feeling triggered (use sheet attached)

_____

_____

_____

_____

_____

Reactive thoughts (based on beliefs, use attached)

_____

_____

_____

_____

_____

Challenge thoughts as follows:

What is **Fact?** (Based on HERE and NOW)

_____

_____

_____ _____

_____

_____

What is **Fiction?** (Based on your story, i.e., the past)

_____

_____

_____

_____

_____

Self-Affirmation that Replaces Reactive Thought

_____

_____

_____

_____

_____

Reactive Thinking That Feeds the Delusions

1. All-or-none...Black-or-white
2. Overgeneralizing
3. Dwelling on the negative
4. Discounting the positive
5. Jumping to conclusions
6. Blowing out of proportion or exaggerating
7. "Should" statements
8. Labeling
9. Judging
10. Self-blame or blaming others

Mindfulness Practices

Here are simple phrases you can use to bring you back to the present while meditating.

1. "Am I Sure?" Misperceptions are a major cause of suffering. Ask yourself if your perceptions and views reflect reality, or if they are based upon misperceptions, opinions, and unskillful thinking.

2. "What Am I Doing?" Use this question as a bell of mindfulness to bring you back to the present moment. Often we are so caught up in the past or future that we miss what is happening now.

3. "Where Am I?" Very similar to "What Am I Doing?" We can get so caught up in thoughts that we get lost in them. This one is especially helpful while sitting. Where are you? Sitting on your cushion and breathing.

4. "Hello, Habit Energy." Through our lifetime, we develop habitual patterns of conditioning. We tend to stick to these habits, even when they cause us to suffer. Noticing them when they occur, and simply acknowledging them without guilt (and that's the important part) lessens their power over us.

5. Bodhichitta. This is a Buddhist term for the deep aspiration to cultivate the understanding in us that inspires us to work to bring happiness to all beings. It is the motivating force for the practice of mindful living.

Fabricating Stories/Adding Things

This is often caused by fear and insecurity. For example, you are waiting to meet someone who is late. You start by getting annoyed, progress to thinking about how inconsiderate they are and how inconvenienced you are, and then to being sure they are intentionally late to spite you. Then when more time goes by, you start to worry, imagining all the terrible things that could have befallen them.

Strategy: Ask yourself, "Am I sure?" or "What am I doing?" to help bring you back to the reality of the moment. In the example above, all you know for sure is that your friend is late.

Speculating

Sometimes insights do arise during meditation that lead to great ideas. But it is important not to get caught up in speculation—repeating and refining this idea and trying to hold on to it. If it is a truly great insight, it is there with you. You don't have to keep elaborating on it.

Strategy: Come back to the breath and to the experience of life in this moment of meditation.

Planning

During meditation we can find ourselves repeatedly going over our schedules and plans. We make lists, organize our calendars, and think of all the things we'd like to do. Of course planning is useful, but it also has the potential to separate us from the present in order to try to control the future, preventing us from trusting in life and ourselves.

Strategy: With awareness, come back to the object of your concentration. There is no need to plan anything for the next ten, twenty, or thirty minutes. Just be.

Judging

Evaluating everything (including ourselves) as good, bad, right, or wrong puts us in a state of constantly commenting on life instead of participating fully in it, whatever happens. We even judge our judging, which only adds to an already heavy burden.

Strategy: Come back to the breath and to the authenticity of this moment, just as it is, whether that's hot, cold, quiet, noisy, possibly unpleasant, and on and on. Can you just feel and experience without attaching yourself to the sensation or to its quality?

Calculating

Counting and measuring serve as time-fillers. You calculate how many days until you go on vacation, how much money you need to save up for that new purchase, how many pairs of shoes you have.

Strategy: Remember what you are doing. Return to your object of concentration.

Procrastination

We put things off (especially practice) until conditions are just right: If the house was quieter, or the instructions were better, or if I were seeing results, I would meditate. We cause ourselves so much suffering with "if only."

Strategy: Recognize that now is the only moment. This is the only breath.

Strategy for working with Habitual Thoughts: Don't focus on them directly. Return to your object of concentration and when you notice a distraction arising, simply name it (planning, judging, daydreaming) and come back to your object. Meditation will allow you to see your habits of mind without giving into them. Don't be upset by your habits, just recognize them and return to your meditation, over and over again. This will allow the mind to relax and eventually smooth out those grooves of old habits and create a new groove of awareness and attention.

Occupying Thoughts

These are the relatively light ones, those trains of thought that start with thinking about lunch and end up all the way back at your junior high romance, with no idea how you got there. Making lists is another type. Occupying thoughts don't usually have a strong pull on our feelings or emotions. They are just things that give the mind something to do and usually are what happen when the mind is left to roam at will.

Strategy: It's important to remember that meditation requires a certain amount of discipline. We are not just sitting and filling time; we are training the mind to become more alert in a gentle yet determined way.

Working with Thoughts

There is a common misunderstanding that meditation is about stopping the thoughts. That's impossible! Thoughts are the natural activity of the mind. Meditation provides the opportunity to observe the thoughts and to help us relate differently to them so that we are no longer dominated by them. The meditation teacher Martine Batchelor categorizes thoughts into three types: occupying (discussed above), intense, and habitual.

Intense Thoughts

These are the thoughts that arise under the influence of shock and pain. They are hard to deal with because they are so powerful and disturbing, and they have the potential to carry us away.

Strategy: When they arise, try to remind yourself that repeating these thoughts is not helpful, that you are just making the situation more intense. Try to create space in your mind by increasing your effort to concentrate on the object of your attention.

Habitual Thoughts

These are grooves we form in our mind by repeating them over and over. There are many subcategories, including:

Daydreaming

Daydreams or fantasies usually form around the idea of something we would like—whether it's an object or a situation. This thought pattern is a very enticing one because not only do we get to write, direct, and star in our own movie, the ending always comes out the way we want it to! There are endless ways to tweak the daydream, making it a never-ending source of entertainment for the mind.

Strategy: Remember that daydreams are one-dimensional, and that multifaceted reality will never fit into them! Concentrate on the breath and come back to reality.

Remembering/Going Over the Past

Another common tendency of the mind is to obsess over things that have happened in the past. We go back and replay the scenario over and over, and then begin adding the "if onlys" and "I should haves." Sometimes we let this project into the future so we can envision what will occur "next time this happens."

Strategy: Recognize that the past is gone and no longer exists. Can you learn from it? Can you let it go instead of dragging it into the present and recreating pain?

Taken from Rev. Laura Bonyon Neal at the Commit to Sit Retreat at the True Nature Zen Center in Bar Harbor, Maine. Contact info: yoga@cattitude.com